ORIGAMI
LONDON

MARK BOLITHO

axis ● books

ORIGAMI
LONDON

MARK BOLITHO

axis ● books

Published in the United Kingdom 2012
by Axis Books Limited
8c Accommodation Road
London NW11 8ED

www.axisbooks.co.uk

Publisher: Siân Keogh
Art Director: Sean Keogh
Designer: Simon DeLotz
Editor: Anna Southgate
Production: Bili Books

ISBN: 978-1-908621-95-5

Printed and bound in China

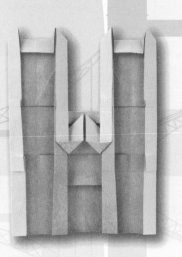

contents

introduction

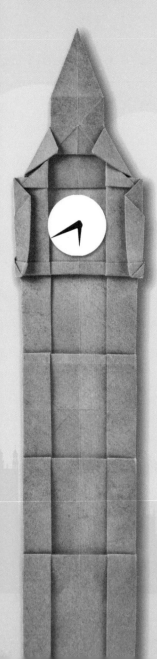

The word 'Origami' is the Japanese word for paper folding and the art is very much associated with Japan. However, there is also a western tradition of paper folding. The Japanese name was adopted by origami societies outside Japan in the 1950s and it soon became the internationally recognised name for the art of folding paper.

Paper folding is a practice that has emerged over time and is probably as old as paper itself. The craft has emerged through the ages, from traditional designs passed between generations to sophisticated complex designs that have been invented in the last fifty years. The reasons for the recent developments in technical design may be due to early manufactured paper not being as malleable as its present day equivalent. The quality of paper produced would have limited the level of technical complexity that could be achieved. As paper technology advanced, larger thinner sheets of paper could be produced and new folding possibilities realised.

There are no strict rules in paper folding. However, there is a school of thought that advocates a classic origami style requiring a model to be made from an uncut square. Most of the models in this collection are made from squares of paper. However, breaking from this constraint, some of the models are made from rectangles and some are made from multiple sheets. A successful origami design will capture the essential characteristics of the object it represents. Buildings are a particular challenge. A successful origami building will capture an element of the object it represents. This may be the shape or a particular architectural feature.

Origami London is a collection of paper folded landmarks of London. The models have been designed and grouped into sections based on the function and purpose of the buildings. Within the collection various categories of building have been included, from iconic offices to museums. The models are explained with step by step diagrams using a standard notation. The illustrations explain the folding sequence to produce the final design. The satisfaction of origami comes not only from creating interesting designs, but also from following the folding journey and seeing your model evolve at your fingertips. Hopefully this will inspire you to further creativity,through your choice of paper to execute the models. Try experimenting by modifying the models presented or creating your own designs.

I hope that you enjoy folding them as much as I enjoyed designing them.

folds and symbols

Origami instructions take you through a step by step process from start to finish. The process uses symbols to explain the transition from one step to the next. Each step shows how the folded project should look and it shows the folds that should be applied to move to the next step.

The challenge of origami diagrams is to explain the folding process. This is done by describing two possible folds. The valley fold creates a crease that folds away from the observer or makes a V shape. The mountain fold comes towards the observer and makes an opposite V shape. More advanced folds can be produced by combining these two folds.

The illustration below demonstrates mountain and valley folds. It also shows how arrows are used to describe the folding process.

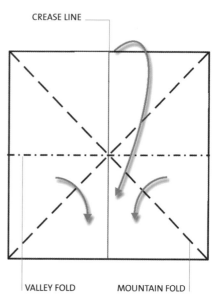

CREASE LINE

VALLEY FOLD   MOUNTAIN FOLD

arrows indicate the direction of the fold

MOUNTAIN FOLD

VALLEY FOLD

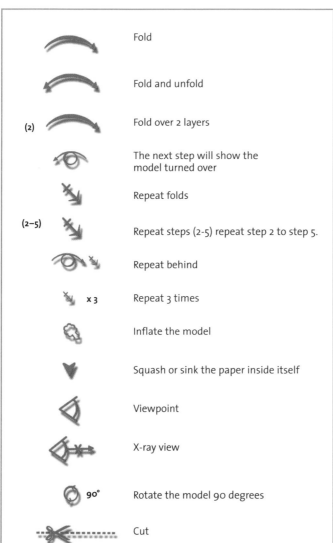

Fold

Fold and unfold

(2)   Fold over 2 layers

The next step will show the model turned over

Repeat folds

(2–5)   Repeat steps (2-5) repeat step 2 to step 5.

Repeat behind

x 3   Repeat 3 times

Inflate the model

Squash or sink the paper inside itself

Viewpoint

X-ray view

90°   Rotate the model 90 degrees

Cut

This symbol is used to highlight a reference point in the folding process

FOLDING TIPS

Follow the steps in numbered order, one at a time.

Look out for the reference points, both in the step you are trying to complete and also by look ahead to see how the model should look when the fold is completed.

Fold as accurately as possible. If the step requires you to fold the model in half, look around the fold and match the reference points indicated, align these points, then make the crease.

You should fold on a level surface. You can fold in the air, but it is easier to make clean accurate folds when working on something flat.

following instructions

The instructions are in two colours. The coloured side represents the front of the paper and the white side the underside. When using patterned paper, treat the coloured side as the patterned side.

The diagrams for each design show the construction process broken down into steps that present one or two folds in the process. Each diagram shows a stage of the model and explains how to move to the next step. By following the numbered instructions you will be able to move through the steps and complete the project. Before attempting a step, make sure that the model you are making looks like the step diagram. Look ahead to the next stage to see what the model will look like after the folds have been applied. Each step shows where to make each fold with either mountain or valley fold lines. Arrows indicate the direction of each fold and the caption below gives an extra commentary on the folds required. When the step is completed the model should look like the image in the next step. If your model does not resemble the step stage you may have missed a fold, so try working back until you can match your model to a previous step.

EXAMPLE

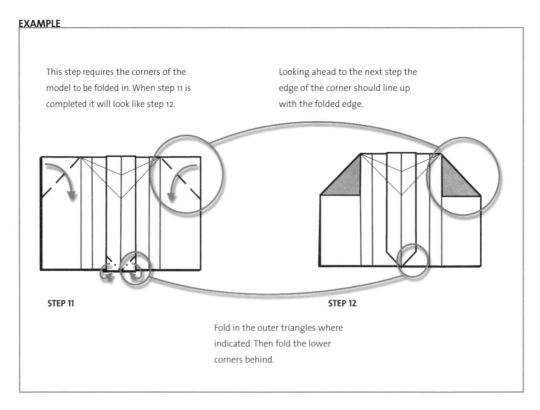

This step requires the corners of the model to be folded in. When step 11 is completed it will look like step 12.

Looking ahead to the next step the edge of the corner should line up with the folded edge.

STEP 11

STEP 12

Fold in the outer triangles where indicated. Then fold the lower corners behind.

MAKING A SQUARE

Folded models can be made from any shape of paper. However, origami is associated with folding paper squares and most of the projects in this book start from a square. You can buy pre-cut squares, or you can use the following technique to make a square from a rectangle.

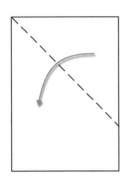
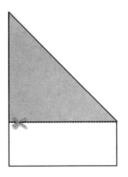
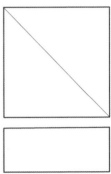

1 Fold over the top edge so that it is lined up with the left side.

2 Holding the folded edge to the paper. Cut along the folded line using the folded edge as a ruler.

3 Then separate the two parts. You now have a square to start folding and a residual rectangle.

MAKING AN 2 X 1 RECTANGLE

The following method shows how to make a 2 x 1 rectangle from a any standard rectangular sheet of paper.

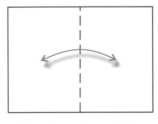
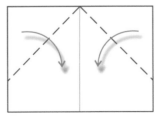
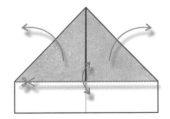

1 Fold and score then unfold along the middle.

2 Fold the outer edges in to align the upper edges with the middle crease.

3 Fold up along the edges of the folded triangles and cut along the crease. The top section will be a 2 x 1 rectangle.

materials and equipment

MARKER PEN

Although the bone folder is designed for folding, other everyday items such as marker pens can be used to press sharper creases.

CHOPSTICK

A chopstick can be useful for manipulating the inside of a model, particularly to work on detail and create points.

GUILLOTINE

These are good for cutting long straight edges. The design of the product enables cutting at right angles.

SCISSORS

A good pair of scissors is invaluable for cutting paper. The best scissors for the task will have long straight blades.

BONE FOLDER

Various devices can be used to enhance folding. The so called "bone folder" is a product used in the bookbinding industry, they can be used to enhance a crease by applying pressure along a fold. Although originally made from bone, they are now available in plastic.

BONE FOLDER   SCISSORS   CHOPSTICKS   GUILLOTINE

PAPER

As origami is all about folding paper, the choice of paper is an important part of the process. All paper can be folded. However, paper composition can affect its ability to hold a crease which impacts its suitability to be used to create folded models. A paper's suitability depends on the quality and thickness of the paper used. If paper is too thick it may break when a fold is applied as the fibres are strained in the process. If the paper has a greater elasticity it may not be able to hold a crease when folded. Paper manufacture is a technical process. When paper is produced it is classified by its weight. This is a specification called gsm, or 'grams per square metre'. This specification gives a weight of a square metre of the paper. This is an important consideration as the higher the weight, or gsm, the thicker the paper will be. For folded paper projects generally the thinner the paper the better. However, for larger projects it may be worth investigating papers with a higher weight as it may enhance the structure of the final model.

The most suitable paper is a lightweight paper with a high malleability that will hold a crease when folded. Choice of colour is also important from a design perspective and should be a consideration before embarking on a project. Lighter colours will show off creases better and natural colours will create a more organic feel to the final model. Patterned papers can be particularly effective and you can create beautiful designs using Japanese washi paper.

Specific origami paper can be purchased. It is generally available in 15 cm squares, and is readily available in a wide variety of colours and patterns. Its weight is about 70 gsm. However, if you cannot obtain origami paper, paper of a weight up to 100 gsm is just as suitable for most origami projects.

All paper can be folded, but choosing the right paper to create your origami models can make a huge difference to the finished piece. If the paper is too thick it can tear when folded, too elastic and it will not hold the creases.

the models

cleopatra's needle

An Egyptian obelisk made of red granite, it stands about 21 metres (68 feet) high. The 180-ton needle originally came from the ancient city of Heliopolis and was believed to have been erected by order of Pharaoh Thutmose III around 1450 BC.

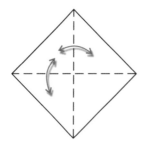

1 Start with a square white side down. Fold and unfold the square diagonally.

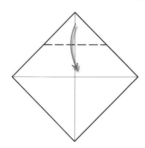

2 Fold the upper corner to the middle of the square.

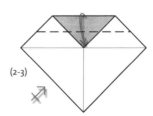

(2-3)

3 Fold the edge over again to the middle. Repeat steps 2-3 on the lower section.

4 Fold the corner in on the left-hand side of the model.

5 Fold and unfold the edges to the middle. Rotate the model 90 degrees.

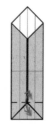

6 Fold and unfold the lower edge at the tip of the folded triangle.

7 Fold the top section down and back up again making a pleat.

8 Fold the edge in at a slight diagonal as indicated.

9 Slide the top of the base out slightly while holding the upper folded edge.

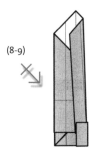

(8-9)

10 Repeat steps 8-9 on the other side, try to make the fold identical to the previous one.

London's obelisk, near Victoria Embankment Gardens in London, was presented to the city by Mehemet Ali, the then-viceroy of Egypt, in 1819 but remained in Alexandria for nearly 60 years until the British government could afford to move it. The cost of bringing the needle to London was £10,000.

Egyptian hieroglyphs cover the structure and experts note that these were added about 200 years later by Ramesses II in honour of his military victories.

Two bronze replicas of Egyptian sphinxes sit on either side of Cleopatra's Needle and bear the inscription 'the good god, Thuthmosis III given life', written in hieroglyphics. Other Egyptian-style touches adorn the embankment where the obelisk sits.

Though the needle was restored in 2005, damage can still be seen on one of the sphinxes' pedestal, caused when a German bomb landed near it during a World War I air raid.

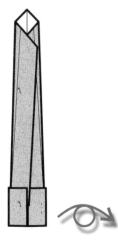

11 Turn the model over. Open the folded edges behind out to make a base for the model to stand on.

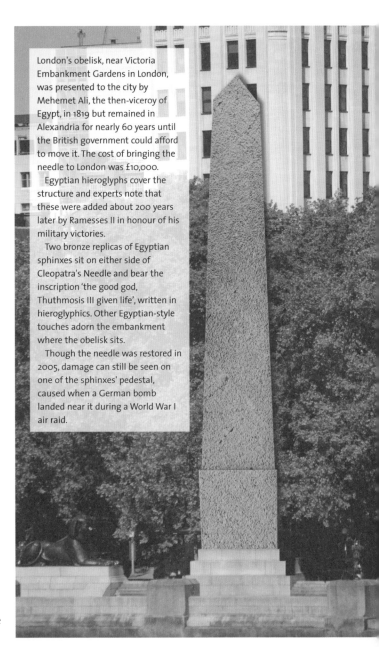

the monument

The Monument stands at the junction of Monument Street and Fish Street Hill in the City of London. It was built between 1671 and 1677 to commemorate the Great Fire of London and to celebrate the rebuilding of the City.

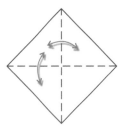

1 Start with a square coloured side down. Fold and unfold the square diagonally.

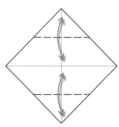

2 Fold and unfold the upper and lower corners to the middle of the square.

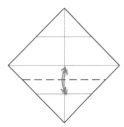

3 Fold and unfold between the creases indicated.

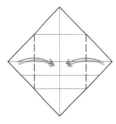

4 Fold the corners on either side to the middle.

5 Fold the edges on either side to the middle.

6 Fold the edges on either side to the middle again.

7 Fold the lower corner up. Turn the model over.

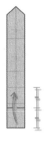

8 Fold the lower section up so that the lower edge touches the second crease.

9 Fold the lower section back down to the lower edge. Fold the top section over along the crease indicated.

10 Fold and unfold the top between the upper edge and the top of the white diamond.

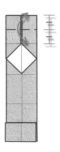

11 Fold and unfold the top layer between the upper edge and the crease made previously.

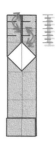

12 Fold and unfold the top layer of the upper section between the creases indicated.

13 Fold the upper section up along the crease indicated.

14 Turn the model over. Fold and unfold the outer corners.

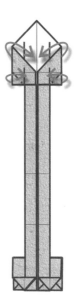

15 Fold the edges to the middle and fold in the outer corners.

16 Fold the top section down and then up again, to make a pleat.

17 Fold the edges of the top section to the middle. Flatten the lower corners.

the monument continued

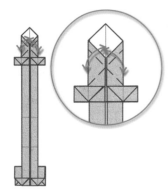

18 In the top section, fold and unfold the outer edges to the folded edge below.

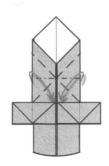

19 Fold the top section down and reverse the edges in to the middle.

20 Fold and unfold the edges and the top corner in where indicated.

21 Fold the top layer up. This will cause the outer edges to fold behind.

22 Fold the outer edges in. Turn the model over.

23 Fold the top layer of the lower section up.

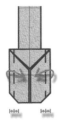

24 Fold the edges of the lower section in as indicated.

25 Fold the lower section back down again.

26 Pull the edges of the lower section apart to make a more stable base.

The Great Fire of London began in a baker's house in Pudding Lane on Sunday 2nd September 1666 and was finally extinguished on Wednesday 5th September, after destroying the greater part of the City. As part of the rebuilding, it was decided to erect a permanent memorial of the Great Fire near the place where it began. Sir Christopher Wren, the architect of St. Paul's Cathedral, and his friend, Dr Robert Hooke, provided a design for a colossal Doric column containing a cantilevered stone staircase of 311 steps leading to a viewing platform. On the very top was a drum and a copper urn from which flames emerged, symbolising the Great Fire. The Monument, as it came to be called, is 61 metres high (202 feet) - the exact distance between it and the site in Pudding Lane where the fire began.

The column was completed in 1677, and Wren's original intention, was to use it for certain experiments of the Royal Society, but vibrations caused by ceaseless traffic proved too great for the success of these experiments and they were discontinued. The Monument became a place of historic interest, unique of its kind, providing visitors with an opportunity to look across London in all directions from a height of about 160 feet, being the level of the public gallery.

the shard

The Shard is the tallest building in Western Europe, its glass façade transforming the London skyline with a mixed-use 310 m (1,016 ft) vertical city of offices, restaurants, a 5-star hotel, residential apartments and the capital's highest viewing gallery offering 360° views.

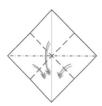

1 Fold and unfold a square lengthwise and diagonally. Refold the creases to form a base.

2 Fold in the outside edges to the middle. Then fold over the top triangle. Then unfold.

3 Fold the front layer up along the crease made in step 2. This will cause the outer edges to fold behind.

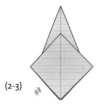

(2-3)

4 Turn the model over. Repeat steps 2 to 3.

5 Fold the front layer to the other side.

6 Fold the lower corner up to meet the crease in the middle.

7 Fold the outer edges in between the top point and the corner made by the folded corner.

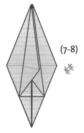

(7-8)

8 Repeat steps 7 to 8 on the other side of the model.

9 Separate the upper corners slightly. Then open the lower section slightly to make a base.

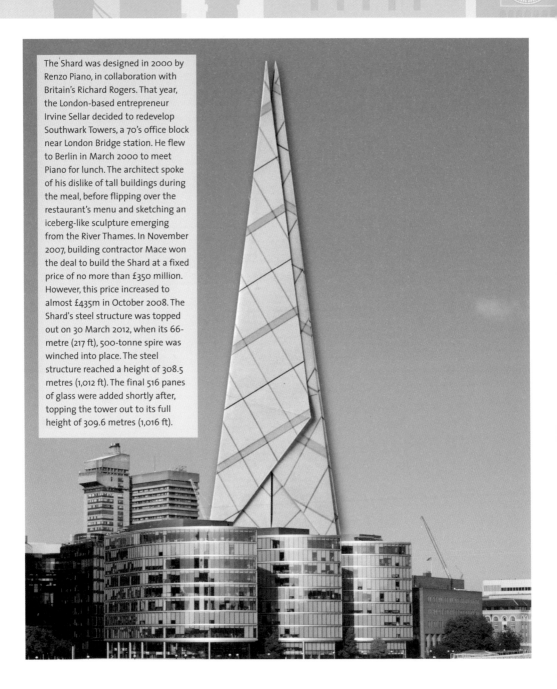

The Shard was designed in 2000 by Renzo Piano, in collaboration with Britain's Richard Rogers. That year, the London-based entrepreneur Irvine Sellar decided to redevelop Southwark Towers, a 70's office block near London Bridge station. He flew to Berlin in March 2000 to meet Piano for lunch. The architect spoke of his dislike of tall buildings during the meal, before flipping over the restaurant's menu and sketching an iceberg-like sculpture emerging from the River Thames. In November 2007, building contractor Mace won the deal to build the Shard at a fixed price of no more than £350 million. However, this price increased to almost £435m in October 2008. The Shard's steel structure was topped out on 30 March 2012, when its 66-metre (217 ft), 500-tonne spire was winched into place. The steel structure reached a height of 308.5 metres (1,012 ft). The final 516 panes of glass were added shortly after, topping the tower out to its full height of 309.6 metres (1,016 ft).

the gherkin

30 St Mary Axe, better known by its nickname *the gherkin*, is one of the most eye-catching buildings in London.

The 41 story skyscraper was built in 2004 and is a modern glass and steel design by the architectural firm of Foster and Partners. Even before its construction was complete Londoners dubbed the building the 'Gherkin' for its distinctive shape, and it is still known by that name.

The tower was built on the site of the 1903 Baltic Exchange Building which had been damaged by a terrorist attack in 1992.

The structure has a steel frame with circular floor plans and a glass facade with diamond-shaped panels. The swirling striped pattern visible on the exterior is the result of the building's energy-saving system which allows the air to flow up through spiraling wells. On the street level, the Gherkin's base is well integrated with an open public plaza. Huge white X braces create a dramatic entrance. The top of the tower, where visitors find an open hall covered by a glass conical dome is even more spectacular. From here you have great views over the city. Unfortunately the building is not open to the public.

Its unique, bold and energy efficient design has won the Gherkin many awards including the Stirling Prize, the London Region Award, and the Emporis Skyscraper Award.

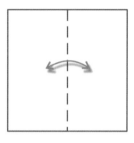

1 Start with a square coloured side down. Fold and unfold the square lengthwise.

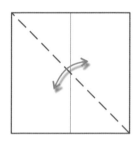

2 Now neatly fold and unfold diagonally.

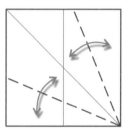

3 Fold and unfold the outer and lower edges to the middle.

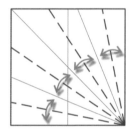

4 Fold and unfold between the creases indicated.

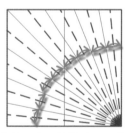

5 Fold and unfold between the creases indicated.

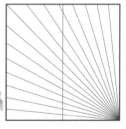

6 Repeat steps 2 to 5 on the other side.

7 Fold the upper corner in so that the outer edge touches the crease indicated.

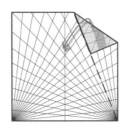

8 Fold the outer corner over again along the crease.

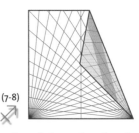

(7-8)

9 Repeat steps 7-8 on the other side of the model.

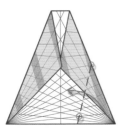

10 Fold the lower corner in. The fold should go through the points indicated.

11 Fold the corner back. The upper edge should touch the outer folded edge.

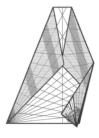

12 Fold and unfold the corner of the lower section.

13 Fold the lower point up and reverse the fold made in the previous step.

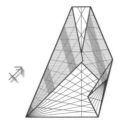

14 Repeat steps 10 to 13 on the other side.

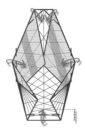

15 Fold the top corners in. Then fold in the outer and lower edges where indicated.

the gherkin continued

16 Fold the lower points back down. This will form a base for the model.

17 Turn the model over. Fold out the triangles behind to make a base for the model to stand on.

the royal exchange

The Royal Exchange in the City of London was founded in 1565 by Sir Thomas Gresham to act as a centre of commerce for the city and was officially opened by Queen Elizabeth I who awarded the building its Royal title on 23 January 1571.

1 Fold and unfold the square in half lengthwise along both axes.

2 Fold and unfold the outer edges to the middle.

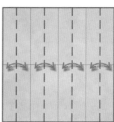

3 Fold and unfold between the creases. This will divide the paper into eight sections.

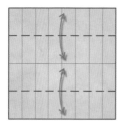

4 Fold and unfold the upper and lower edge to the middle line.

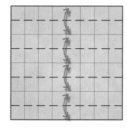

5 Fold and unfold between the creases indicated.

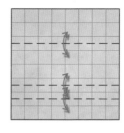

6 Fold and unfold between the creases.

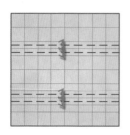

7 Fold and unfold between the creases indicated.

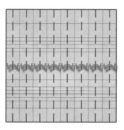

8 Fold and unfold between the creases indicated. This divides the paper into sixteen sections.

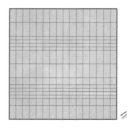

9 Now turn the model over from left to right.

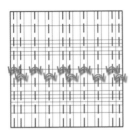

10 Fold and unfold between the creases indicated.

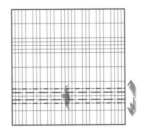

11 Fold up and down along the creases indicated causing the upper and lower creases to touch.

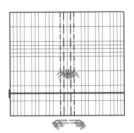

12 Fold the middle section along the creases indicated causing the outer creases to touch.

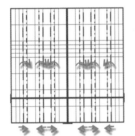

13 Repeat the pleating process where indicated.

14 Repeat this process where indicated. Making two lengthwise pleats.

15 Fold the corner over between the opposite corner and the folded edge of the upper section.

16 Fold the left outer corner over as indicated.

17 Fold both the outer edges in to the line indicated.

18 Fold the lower edge up as shown.

the royal exchange continued

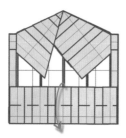

19 Fold the lower edge back down again. This will form a base to support the model.

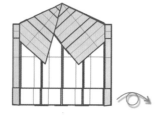

20 Turn the model over. It is now complete.

Gresham's original building was destroyed in the Great Fire of London in 1666. The second was also destroyed by fire on 10 January 1838.

The third Royal Exchange building, which still stands today, was designed by Sir William Tite and follows the original layout - a four-sided structure surrounding a central courtyard where merchants and tradesmen could do business. The internal works were designed by Edward I'Anson in 1837. It was opened by Queen Victoria in 1844.

The Royal Exchange ceased to act as a centre of commerce in 1939, although it was, for a few years in the 1980s, home to the London International Financial Futures Exchange (LIFFE). It is now a luxurious shopping centre.

the albert hall

Opened by Queen Victoria in 1871, the Albert Hall has become one of the UK's most treasured and distinctive buildings. Hosting over 350 events a year, from classical, rock and pop concerts, to ballet and opera, sports, award ceremonies and charity events.

After the success of the Great Exhibition in 1851, Prince Albert proposed building a series of permanent facilities the Albert Hall being one of them Unfortunately he died before seeing any of his plans come to fruition. It was originally going to be called The Central Hall of Arts and Sciences, but the name was changed by Queen Victoria to Royal Albert Hall of Arts and Sciences when laying the foundation stone as a dedication to her deceased husband Prince Albert. It forms the practical part of a national memorial to the Prince Consort – the decorative part is the Albert Memorial directly to the north in Kensington Gardens, now separated from the Hall by the road Kensington Gore.

The official opening ceremony of the Hall was on 29 March 1871. A welcoming speech was given by Edward, the Prince of Wales as Queen Victoria was too overcome to speak. A concert followed which was when the halls acoustic problems became apparent.

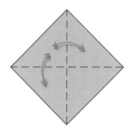

1 Start with a square coloured side up. Fold and unfold the square diagonally.

2 Fold and unfold the corner to the middle of the square.

3 Fold and unfold between the creases. This divides the upper section into four sections.

4 Fold and unfold between the creases. This divides the upper section into eight sections.

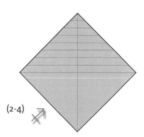

(2-4)

5 Repeat steps 2 to 4 on the lower section.

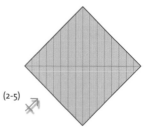

(2-5)

6 Rotate the model 90 degrees. Repeat steps 2 to 5.

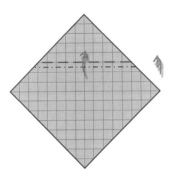

7 Fold the square up along the crease indicated. Then back again. This will cause an edge to fold upwards.

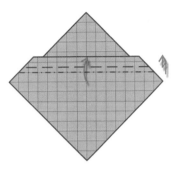

8 Repeat the folding method from the previous step where indicated. Turn the model over.

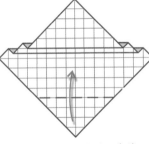

9 Fold the lower corner up to touch the centre line of the square.

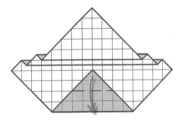

10 Fold the point back down again to touch the outer edge.

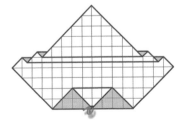

11 Fold the tip of the centre lower folded triangle behind as shown.

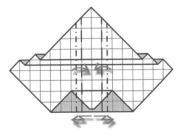

12 Fold the sides in along the crease and back again. This will cause two parallel pleats.

the albert hall continued

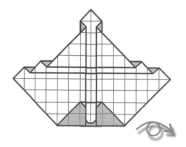

13 Now turn the model over left to right to start folding on the other side.

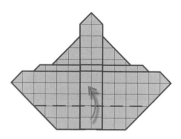

14 Fold the lower section up along the crease indicated.

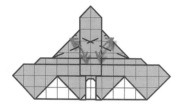

15 Fold and unfold the upper section. Folding the outer edge over to the folded edge.

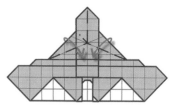

16 Make both folds made in the previous step together, this will cause the upper point to fold in half.

17 Fold the corner up as shown. Open the layers and then flatten carefully.

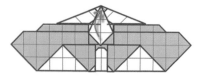

18 Fold the squashed section of the model up as indicated.

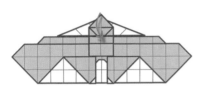

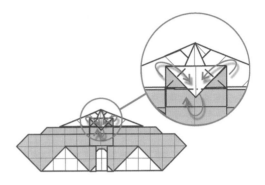

19 Fold the point of the centre section down where indicated.

20 On the top section fold the corners in and the tip behind and into the model.

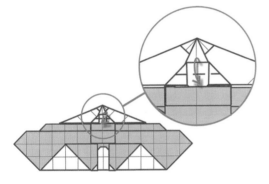

21 Fold the top section in half as shown in the enlarged detail.

22 Hold the middle part and fold the outer edges down, this will cause both of the inner corners in.

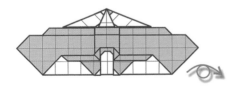

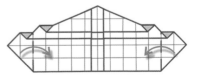

23 Flatten all the folds just made and the turn the model over.

24 Fold both of the outer corners in to the lines indicated by the arrows.

the albert hall continued

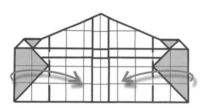

25 Fold both the left and right edges in again to meet the lines indicated by the arrows.

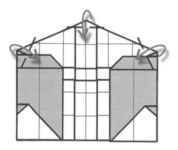

26 Fold the corners in at the top and on the sides to make a more rounded roof shape.

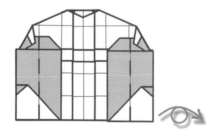

27 Turn the model over. Open the edges behind to enable the model to stand.

Engineers first attempted to solve the strong echo by suspending a canvas awning below the dome. This helped and also sheltered concertgoers from the sun, but the problem was not solved, it used to be said jokingly that the hall was 'the only place where a British composer could be sure of hearing his work twice'.

In 1949 the canvas was removed and the glass dome was replaced with fluted aluminium panels in a new attempt to solve the echo, however, the acoustics were not properly tackled until 1969 when a series of large fibreglass acoustic diffusing discs (commonly referred to as 'mushrooms' or 'flying saucers') were installed below the ceiling to reduce the notorious echo.

the festival hall

The hall was built as part of the Festival of Britain and was officially opened on 3 May 1951. It is the first post-war building to become Grade I protected.

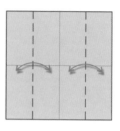

1 Start with the coloured side up. Fold and unfold the square in half lengthwise along both axes.

2 Fold and unfold the outer edges to touch the middle crease line.

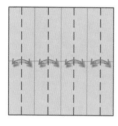

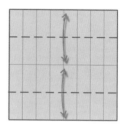

3 Fold and unfold between the creases. This will divide the paper into eight sections.

4 Fold and unfold the upper and lower edge to the middle line.

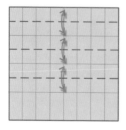

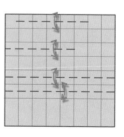

5 Fold and unfold between the creases made in the previous steps.

6 Fold and unfold again between the creases indicated by the arrows.

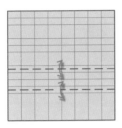

7 Fold and unfold between the creases indicated. Turn the model over.

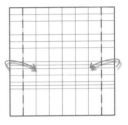

8 Fold outer the edges in along the creases made previously.

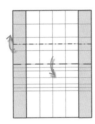

9 Fold the top section down and then back up again where indicated.

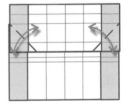

10 Fold and unfold the corners of the middle section to the bounding upper crease.

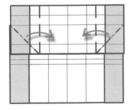

11 Fold the outer edges in and reverse the folds made in the previous step. Turn the model over.

The Hall was taken over by the Arts Council in 1986, Since the late 1980s the hall has operated an 'open foyers' policy, opening up the substantial foyer spaces to the public throughout the day, even if there are no performances. This has proved very popular and the foyers are now one of the most used public spaces in London.

Skateboarders, who have congregated since the 1980s in the undercroft of the neighbouring Queen Elizabeth Hall, considered to be London's most iconic skateboarding area, now constitute a notable feature of the Southbank Centre

the festival hall continued

The hall's design is Modernist, the Festival's commissioning architect, Hugh Casson, took the decision in 1948 to appoint only young architects and the team led by Leslie Martin, Robert Matthew and Peter Moro was from the LCC's Architects' Department. Martin designed the structure as an 'egg in a box', a term he used to describe the separation of the curved auditorium space from the surrounding building and the noise and vibration of the adjacent railway viaduct. Sir Thomas Beecham also used a similar description, calling the building a 'giant chicken coop'.

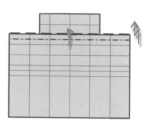

12 Fold the lower section up and then down again to form a pleat.

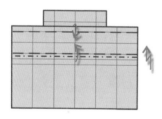

13 Fold the upper edge down along the crease shown. Then fold the lower section up and down making a pleat.

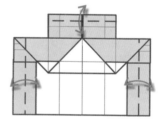

14 Turn the model over. Fold and unfold the outer and top edges in where indicated.

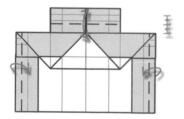

15 Fold the outer edges in to the creases made previously. Then fold and unfold the top section.

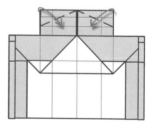

16 Fold the top outer corners in between the mid line and the crease made previously.

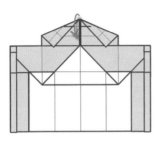

17 Fold over the tip of the top section to the crease made in step 15.

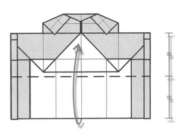

18 Fold the edge of the lower section up to where the point meets the edge above.

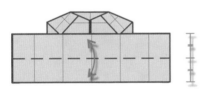

19 Fold and unfold the front section along the middle as indicated.

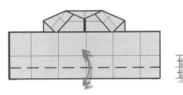

20 Fold and unfold the front section between the lower edge and the crease made previously.

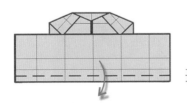

21 Fold down between the lower edge and the crease made previously.

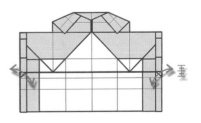

22 Fold and unfold both of the outer corners of the lower section.

the festival hall continued

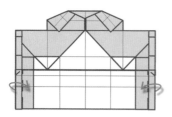

23 Fold the edges of the lower section in and reverse the folds made previously.

24 Fold the lower edge up and back down again to make a stand for the model. Turn the model over and it is complete.

02 arena

Originally named the Millenium Dome, The 02 Arena is the joint largest indoor arena in Europe with a capacity of 23,000, it is used mainly for live music..

PART ONE: THE DOME Start with a square coloured side up.

1 Fold and unfold the square in half diagonally. Then turn the model over.

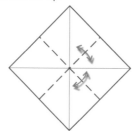

2 Fold and unfold the square in half lengthwise.

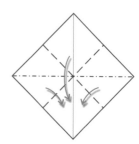

3 Re fold the creases made previously to form a preliminary base.

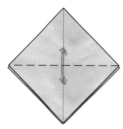

4 Fold and unfold the lower corner up along the middle of the model.

5 Fold and unfold the top corner to the middle as indicated.

6 Fold and unfold the top corner to the crease made previously.

7 Fold and unfold the top corner to the crease made previously.

8 Sink fold the top into the model along the crease just made.

9 Fold the top edge over and open out the edges.

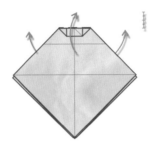

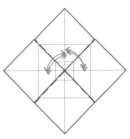

10 Fold the top edge behind as indicated.

11 Open out the model along the edge made from the folded top section.

12 Fold and unfold the model lengthwise.

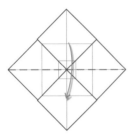

The dome is one of the largest of its type in the world. Externally, it appears as a large white marquee with twelve 100 metre-high yellow support towers, one for each month of the year, or each hour of the clock face, representing the role played by Greenwich Mean Time. In plan view it is circular, 365 metres in diameter, one metre for each day of the year, with scalloped edges. The canopy is made of PTFE-coated glass fibre fabric, a durable and weather-resistant plastic, and is 52 metres high in the middle, one metre for each week of the year. It has become one of the United Kingdom's most recognisable landmarks. It can easily be seen on aerial photographs of London. Its exterior is reminiscent of the Dome of Discovery built for the Festival of Britain in 1951.

13 Rotate the model 90° and fold it in half

14 Fold and unfold the outer edges down to the crease line.

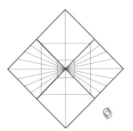

15 Fold and unfold between the creases made previously.

16 Open the model up again. Rotate the model 90°.

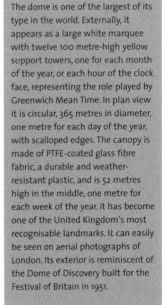

02 arena continued

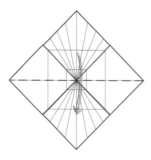

17 Now carefully fold the model in half by folding the upper point down to meet the lower point.

18 Fold and unfold between the creases on both sides as indicated.

19 Fold and unfold between the creases made in the previous step as indicated.

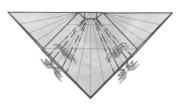

20 Fold the creases in and out again to make two diagonal pleats on both sides.

21 Fold the creases in and out again to make diagonal pleats on both sides in the upper section.

22 Fold the lower section up along the line indicated.

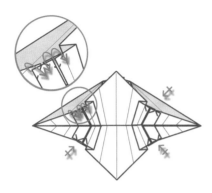

23 Fold the corners over on the corners and repeat those folds where indicated.

The Dome's architect was Richard Rogers and the building structure was engineered by Buro Happold. The entire roof structure weighs less than the air contained within the building. Although referred to as a dome it is not strictly one as it is not self-supporting, but is a mast-supported, dome-shaped cable network. For this reason, it has been disparagingly referred to as the Millennium Tent.

Apart from the dome itself, the project included the reclamation of the entire Greenwich Peninsula. The land was previously derelict and contaminated by toxic sludge from East Greenwich Gas Works that operated from 1889 to 1985.

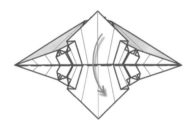

24 Carefully fold the folded section back down again as shown.

25 The dome section of the O2 is now complete, set aside.

PART TWO: THE STEEL MASTS

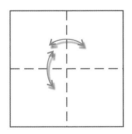

1 Fold and unfold the square in half horizontally and vertically.

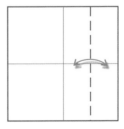

2 Fold and unfold the right hand outer edge to the middle crease.

02 arena continued

Following the closure of the Millennium Experience at the end of 2000, the Millennium Dome was leased for redevelopment as an entertainment complex. This included plans for an indoor arena.

Construction of the arena started in 2003 and finished in 2007. Owing to the impossibility of using cranes inside the dome structure, the arena's roof was constructed on the ground within the dome and then lifted. The arena building's structure was then built around the roof. The arena building, which houses the arena and the arena concourse, is independent from all other buildings in The O2 and houses all the arena's facilities. The whole arena building takes up 40% of the total dome structure.

In 2008, it became the world's busiest venue taking the crown with sales of more than two million tickets per annum.

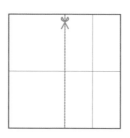

3 Cut the paper along the middle crease.

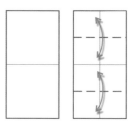

4 Fold and unfold the lower edges to the middle.

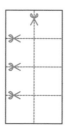

5 Cut along the creases to make eight smaller squares.

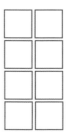

6 You now have the eight smaller squares.

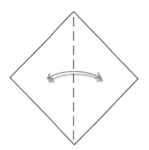

7 Fold and unfold each square in half diagonally.

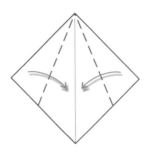

8 Fold the upper edges to the middle.

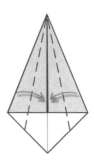

9 Fold the edges in towards the middle again.

10 Fold the lower corners of each mast up.

11 Fold the model in half vertically as shown.

12 Fold and unfold the base of the model.

13 Fold the upper layer up causing the lower corner to fold in.

14 Fold and unfold the lower edge behind.

15 Section complete. You will need to make eight of these.

PART THREE: ASSEMBLING THE MODEL

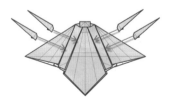

1 Insert the lower edges of 4 masts into the dome. Both sides should be inserted.

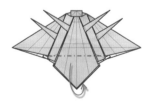

2 Fold the corner behind to lock the model.

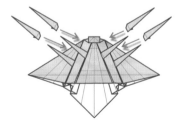

3 Insert the remaining 4 masts behind.

O2 arena continued

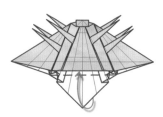

4 Fold the lower edge inside the model.

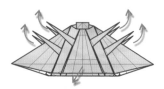

5 Adjust the angle of the spikes. Now open out the dome section.

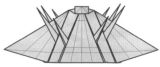

6 The model of the O2 arena is now complete.

westminster abbey

The Collegiate Church of St Peter at Westminster, popularly known as Westminster Abbey, is a large, mainly Gothic church, in the City of Westminster, located just to the west of the Palace of Westminster. It is the traditional place of coronation and burial site for British monarchs and national figures.

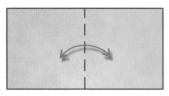

1 Start with a 2 x 1 rectangle. Coloured side up. Fold and unfold along the middle.

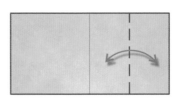

2 Fold and unfold the outer edge to the middle.

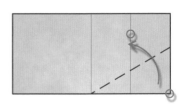

3 Fold the lower corner up from the middle crease. The lower outer corner should touch the crease made previously.

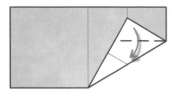

4 Fold the corner back down to the folded edge.

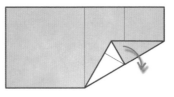

5 Unfold the section back down again as shown.

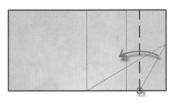

6 Fold the edge over from the point where the crease made previously touches the lower edge.

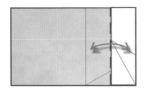

7 Fold and unfold the outer edge to the middle line.

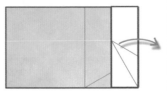

8 Fold the right hand edge back out again.

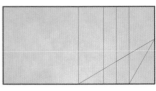

(2-8)

9 Repeat steps 2 to 8 on the other side.

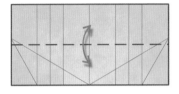

10 Fold and unfold along the middle.

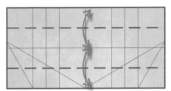

11 Fold and unfold the outer edges to the middle.

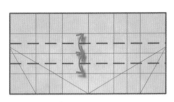

12 Fold and unfold between the creases made previously.

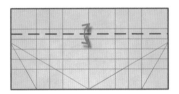

13 Fold and unfold between the creases made previously.

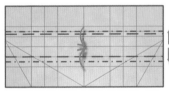

14 Fold the upper and lower sections down and up again along the creases made previously.

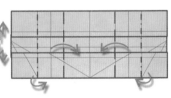

15 Fold the outer sections over and back again along the creases made previously.

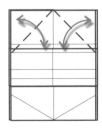

16 Turn over. Fold and unfold the upper corners.

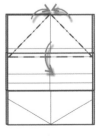

17 Fold the upper section down, fold the corners in and flatten.

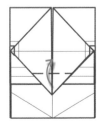

18 Fold the corner up to the crease above.

westminster abbey continued

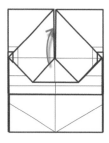

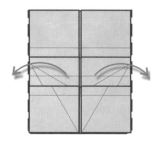

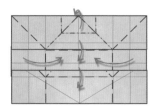

19 Unfold the upper folded section. Turn the model over.

20 Fold the edges out on both sides.

21 Fold the outer edges back in. At the same time refold the middle section to the front. Also fold down the lower edge.

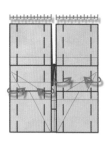

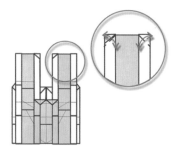

22 Fold the outer edges of the two sections in.

23 The next steps show detail of the top of the towers. Fold and unfold the outer corners.

24 Fold the top edge down and fold in the corner from the previous fold.

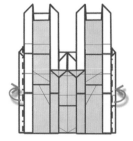

25 Repeat the folds on the other tower.

26 Fold the outer edges behind.

The Abbey dates mainly from the reign of King Henry III. He pulled down the eastern part of the 11th century Abbey in 1245, which had been founded by King Edward the Confessor and dedicated in 1065, to build a more magnificent church in the newest Gothic style. The three master masons supervising the work were Henry of Reyns, who was greatly influenced by the new cathedrals at Reims, Amiens and Chartres, John of Gloucester and Robert of Beverley.

The Abbey has the highest Gothic vault in England (nearly 102 feet) and it was made to seem higher by the narrow aisles. The last phase of building was the completion in 1745 of the West Towers in Portland stone, to a design by Nicholas Hawksmoor, the Abbey's Surveyor.

It is the traditional place of coronation, every monarch since William the Conqueror has been crowned in the Abbey, with the exception of Edward V and Edward VIII who were never crowned, as well as a burial site for monarchs and national figures, from the likes of Geoffrey Chaucer to Admiral Nelson and Sir Winston Churchill. It is also the resting place of the unknown warrior, an unidentified British soldier killed on a European battlefield during the First World war. Of all the graves on the floors of the Abbey this is the only one upon which it is forbidden to tread.

st pauls cathedral

Designed by Sir Christopher Wren the present cathedral is the fifth to have stood on this site since 604, and was built between 1675 and 1710, after the previous cathedral was destroyed in the Great Fire of London.

PART ONE: THE DOME Start with a square coloured side up.

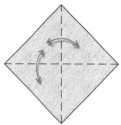

1 Fold and unfold the square diagonally.

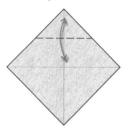

2 Fold and unfold the corner to the middle of the square.

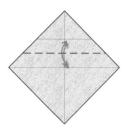

3 Fold and unfold between the creases.

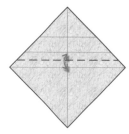

4 Fold and unfold between the creases where indicated.

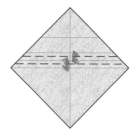

5 Fold and unfold between the creases.

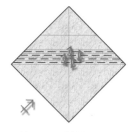

6 Fold and unfold between the creases. Repeat steps 2-6 on the lower section.

7 Rotate the model 90 degrees.

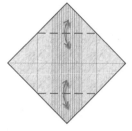

8 Fold and unfold the corners to the middle.

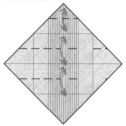

9 Fold and unfold between the creases where indicated.

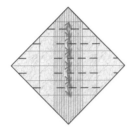

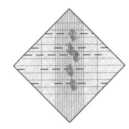

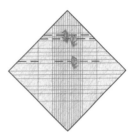

10 Fold and unfold between the creases where indicated.

11 Fold and unfold between the creases where indicated.

12 Fold and unfold between the creases where indicated. turn the model over.

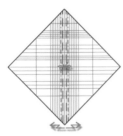

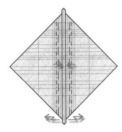

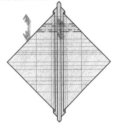

13 Fold the edges in and out again, making a two pleats in the middle. turn the model over.

14 Fold the edges in and out again making two pleats.

15 Fold the top section along the creases made previously, making two pleats and turn over.

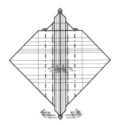

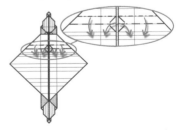

16 Fold the edge in and out again.

17 Neatly fold and unfold the top section.

18 Refold the previous step and fold down the corners of the outer edges of the folded section.

st pauls cathedral continued

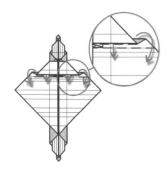

19 Reverse out the lower layer of paper trapped beneath the folded edge.

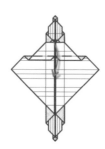

20 Fold the top section over and down as shown.

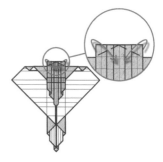

21 Fold the corners of the top section over.

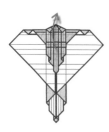

22 Fold the section back up again.

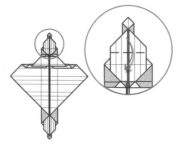

23 Fold the top section down.

24 Fold the section back up again.

25 Fold the corners in and narrow the top point.

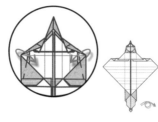

26 Fold the outer edges in. Turn the model over.

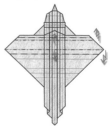

27 Fold the model up and down again along the creases made previously. This will make two pleats. Turn over.

28 Fold the outer edges of the middle section down to the folded edge. This will cause the upper edges to fold over.

29 Fold the lower section up along the crease line.

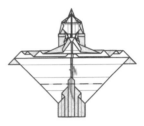

30 Fold the lower section up again where indicated. Turn the model over.

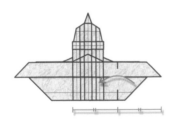

31 Fold the edge over so that the outer corner touches the outer crease in the middle section.

32 Fold the other edge over mirroring the side folded previously.

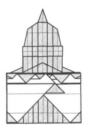

33 Part one of the cathedral is now complete.

PART TWO: THE TOWERS Start with a square coloured side down.

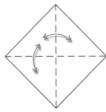

1 Fold and unfold the square diagonally.

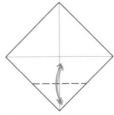

2 Fold and unfold the corner to the middle of the square.

3 Fold between the lower corner and the crease made previously.

st pauls cathedral continued

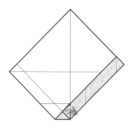

4 Fold and unfold the outer edges of the lower section in.

5 Fold over one edge. At the same time fold lower section over.

6 Fold the corner back as indicated.

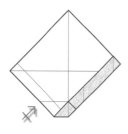

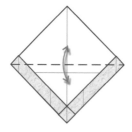

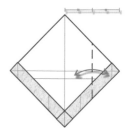

7 Repeat steps 5 to 6 on the other side.

8 Fold and unfold along the middle diagonally.

9 Fold and unfold the outer corner to the middle.

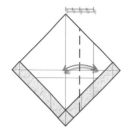

10 Fold and unfold between the crease and the middle.

11 Fold and unfold between the creases.

12 Repeat steps 9 to 11 on the other side.

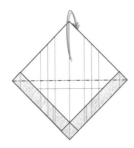

13 Now fold the top section behind.

14 Fold and unfold the corner in to align the edge with the crease.

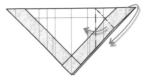

15 Fold the outer corner up, separate the layers, open the point and flatten.

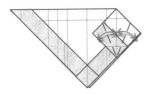

16 Fold and unfold the outer edges in to the middle.

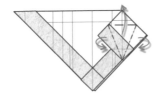

17 Fold the section up and reverse the folds made previously.

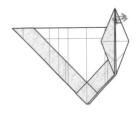

18 Fold over the small folded corner.

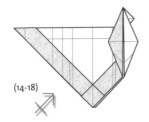

(14-18)

19 Repeat steps 14 to 18 on the other side. Now turn the model over.

20 Fold the lower corner up along the crease line indicated above.

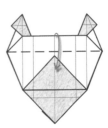

21 Fold the upper edge down to overlap the lower point.

st pauls cathedral continued

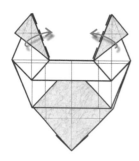

22 Fold both the upper corners out as shown.

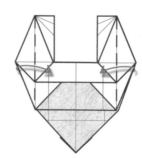

23 Fold the edges on either side in as shown.

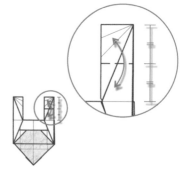

24 Fold and unfold one tower along the middle.

25 Fold and unfold between the outer edges of the section and the middle crease.

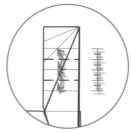

26 Fold and unfold between the creases.

27 Fold the section up and down again, making two pleats.

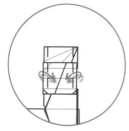

28 Fold the edges in.

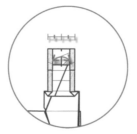

29 Make a short crease along the middle of the top of the tower.

30 Fold the top corners in to the middle.

31 The right hand tower is now complete.

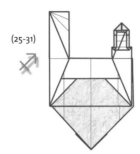

(25-31)

32 Repeat steps 25 to 31 on the other side. Now turn over.

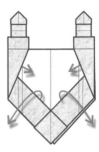

33 Open out the folded section.

34 Fold the top layer up over the two towers .

35 Fold the upper corner down again as shown.

Designed by Sir Christopher Wren the present cathedral is the fifth to have stood on this site since 604, and was built between 1675 and 1710, after the previous cathedral was destroyed in the Great Fire of London. Among the events marked at St Paul's are royal occasions. In 1897 Queen Victoria chose to commemorate her diamond jubilee here. More recently Queen Elizabeth II has celebrated her jubilees at St Paul's , and also her 80th birthday in 2006. Royal weddings have been held here as well: the marriage of Catherine of Aragon to Prince Arthur in 1501 and famously the wedding of HRH the Prince of Wales to Lady Diana Spencer in 1981.

As the nation's church, St Paul's has also been the site of state funerals of British military leaders, including Admiral Lord Nelson, the Duke of Wellington and of the wartime Prime Minister, Sir Winston Churchill.

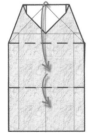

36 Fold the upper section down again twice.

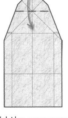

37 Part two of St Pauls cathedral is now complete.

st pauls cathedral continued

ASSEMBLING THE CATHEDRAL

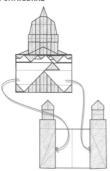

1 Tuck the edges of section one into the pockets beneath the turrets in section two. Set section one in the middle.

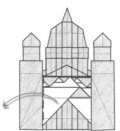

2 Fold the corner of section one out over the edge of the base of the tower of section two.

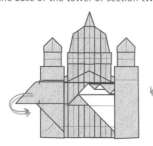

3 Fold the outer corner behind and into the model. Repeat this process on the other folded corner.

st mary le strand

The church stands on what is now a traffic island to the north of Somerset House, at the eastern end of The Strand. It is the official church of the Women's Royal Naval Service, and has a book of remembrance for members who have died in service.

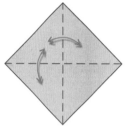

1 Start with a square coloured side up. Fold and unfold the square diagonally.

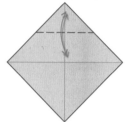

2 Fold and unfold the corner to the middle of the square.

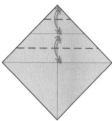

3 Fold and unfold between the creases. This divides the upper section into four.

4 Fold and unfold between the creases. This divides the upper section into eight.

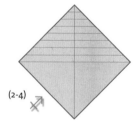

(2-4)

5 Repeat steps 2 to 4 on the lower section.

6 Now rotate the model 90 degrees.

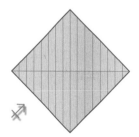

7 Repeat steps 2 to 5 on the other side of the model.

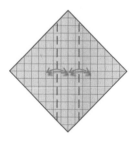

8 Fold and unfold between the creases where indicated.

9 Fold the corner up where indicated. Turn the model over.

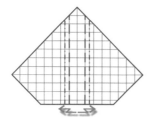

10 Fold the outer sides in and out causing two pleats in the paper.

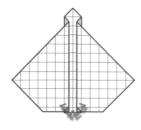

11 Fold and unfold the lower corners as indicated by the arrows.

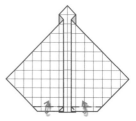

12 Fold the lower edges on either side up. This will reverse the corners folded before.

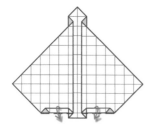

13 Fold the edges back leaving the folded corners. Turn the m

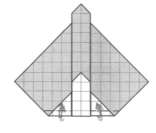

14 Fold the edges up on either side leaving the middle.

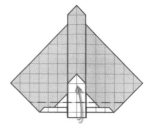

15 Fold the lower section of the model up where indicated.

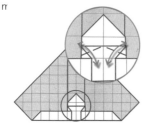

16 Fold and unfold the outer edges of the middle section.

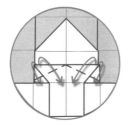

17 Fold both the corners down, then tuck the corners under the layer below.

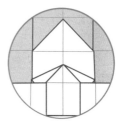

18 The central section of the model is now complete.

st mary le strand continued

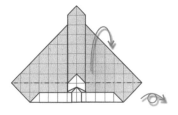

19 Fold the top section behind where indicated. Then turn the model over.

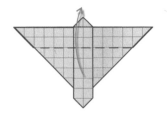

20 Fold the lower section of the model up where indicated.

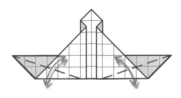

21 Fold and unfold the lower corners on the front layer.

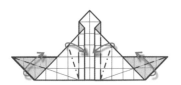

22 Fold the middle section in and fold the two edges up.

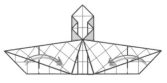

23 Fold both the sides in towards the middle of the model as indicated.

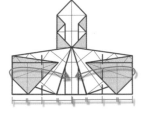

24 Fold the sides in again to the middle.

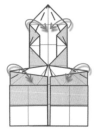

25 Fold the corners of the tower in. Then fold in the corners of the middle section.

26 Now turn the model over to work on the other side .

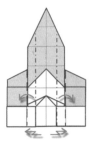

27 Fold the body in and out again forming a raised middle section and narrowing the tower.

The church is the second to have been called St. Mary le Strand, the first having been situated a short distance to the south. The date of its foundation is unclear but it was mentioned in a judgment of 1222, when it was called the Church of the Innocents, or St Mary and the Innocents. It was pulled down in 1549 by Edward Seymour, 1st Duke of Somerset to make way for Somerset House. The new St. Mary le Strand was the first of the fifty new churches built in London under the Commission for Building Fifty New Churches, at a cost of some £16,000. Construction began in February 1714 under the architect James Gibbs, being his first major project following his return from Italy. The steeple was completed in September 1717, but the church was not consecrated for use until 1 January 1723. Bonnie Prince Charlie is alleged to have renounced his Roman Catholic faith in the church to become an Anglican during a secret visit to London in 1750. John Dickens and Elizabeth Barrow, the parents of Charles Dickens, were married here in 1809.

The church narrowly escaped destruction twice during the 20th century. At the turn of the century the London County Council proposed to demolish the church to widen the Strand; but a campaign succeeded in averting this The London Blitz of the Second World War caused much damage to the surrounding area but again the church avoided destruction, though it did suffer damage from a nearby bomb explosion.

victoria and albert museum

The Victoria and Albert Museum (also known as the V&A), is the world's largest museum of decorative arts and design, it houses a collection of over 4.5 million objects. Named after Prince Albert and Queen Victoria, it was founded in 1852.

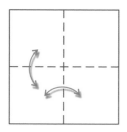

1 Start with a square coloured side down. Fold and unfold the square in half lengthwise.

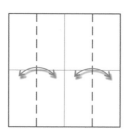

2 Fold and unfold the outer edges to the middle.

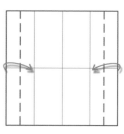

3 Fold the outer edges in to the creases made previously.

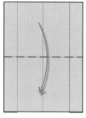

4 Turn the model over and fold the model in half.

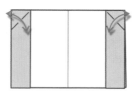

5 Fold and unfold both the left and right hand top corners.

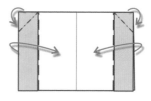

6 Fold the edges in and flatten the outer corners.

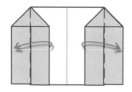

7 Fold the folded edges back on both side if the model.

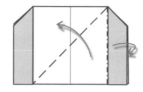

8 Fold the front layer up where indicated. This will cause the outer edge to fold over.

9 Now fold the corner back down as shown.

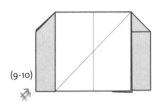

(9-10)

10 Repeat steps 9 to 10 on the other side.

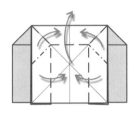

11 Fold the front layer up. At the same time fold in the outer edges.

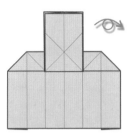

12 The model should now look like this, turn the model over.

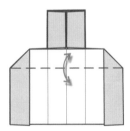

13 Fold and unfold where indicated.

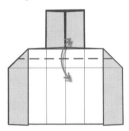

14 Fold and unfold between the folded edge and the crease indicated.

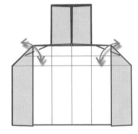

15 Fold and unfold the corners where indicated.

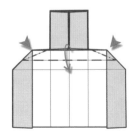

16 Fold the front layer down and flatten the corners.

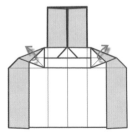

17 Fold out the trapped paper on either side.

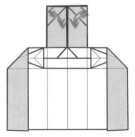

18 Fold and unfold the corners of the top section.

victoria and albert museum continued

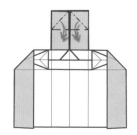

19 Fold the upper edges down reversing the folds made in the previous step.

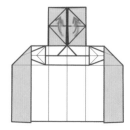

20 Fold the corners made in the top section back up again as shown.

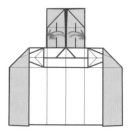

21 In the upper section fold over the upper layer only to fold the edges to the side.

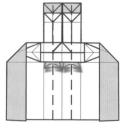

22 Fold and unfold where indicated.

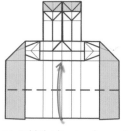

23 Fold the lower edge up to the folded edge above.

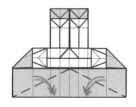

24 Fold the corners of the lower section down between the lower outer corners and the middle.

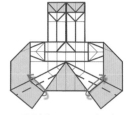

25 Fold the corners back up again. The outer folded edge will then be parallel to both the outer edges.

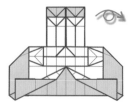

26 Look at what you have before moving on, it should now look like this, turn the model over to work on the other side .

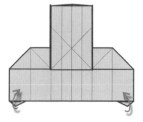

27 Fold the corners up as indicated.

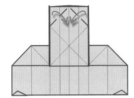

28 Fold the corners of the upper section in to the middle crease line.

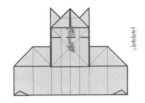

29 Fold and unfold where indicated.

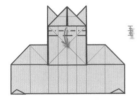

30 Fold the upper section down and up again. This will make a pleat.

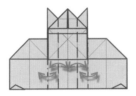

31 Fold and unfold where indicated.

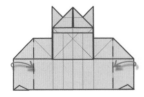

32 Fold both the outer edges in as indicated.

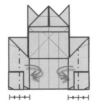

33 Fold the left and right edges behind as indicated to narrow the folded flaps.

The Victoria and Albert Museum's collections span two thousand years of art in almost every medium, from all over the world. The story of the V&A's foundation helps to explain its astonishing richness and diversity.

The Museum was established in 1852, a year after the successful Great Exhibition. The founding principle was to make art available to all, to educate working people and to inspire British designers and manufacturers. The profit from the Great Exhibition was used to set up the Museum of Manufactures, as it was initially known, and exhibits were purchased to form the basis of its collections.

The Museum moved to its present site in 1857 and was renamed the South Kensington Museum. Its collections expanded rapidly as it acquired the best examples of metalwork, furniture, textiles and all other forms of decorative art from all periods. In 1899, Queen Victoria laid the foundation stone of a new building designed to give the Museum a grand façade and main entrance. To mark the occasion, it was renamed the Victoria and Albert Museum, in memory of the enthusiastic support Prince Albert had given to its foundation.

victoria and albert museum continued

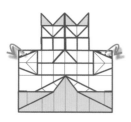

34 Turn the model over. Fold the outer corners behind.

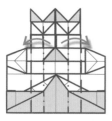

35 Fold the model along the crease made previously to shape the model. This will fold out the middle section. The model is complete.

tate modern

The most visited modern art gallery in the world. The former power station is famous for its Turbine hall, which once housed the electricity generators, and now has become a dramatic entrance and display area for specially commissioned works of contemporary art.

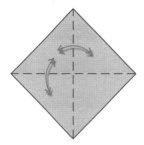

1 Start with a square coloured side up. Fold and unfold the square diagonally.

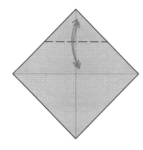

2 Fold and unfold the corner to the middle of the square.

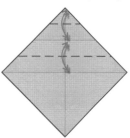

3 Fold and unfold between the creases. This divides the upper section into four.

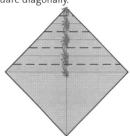

4 Fold and unfold between the creases. This divides the upper section into eight.

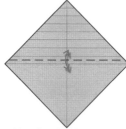

5 Fold and unfold between the lower creases.

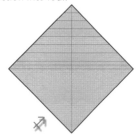

6 Repeat steps 2 to 5 on the lower section.

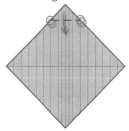

7 Rotate the model 90 degrees. Fold over the tip between the creases where indicated.

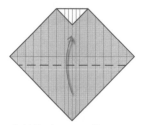

8 Fold the lower section up so that the tip touches the upper folded edge.

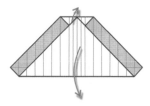

9 Make a crease and then fold back into a square.

10 Fold and unfold the tip to the crease.

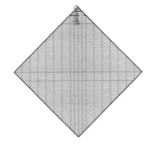

11 Fold the upper tip down to meet the crease and then fold the tip over.

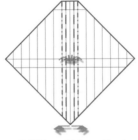

12 Now turn the model over so the pattern is facing down.

13 Fold the middle section in and out again making two pleats.

In December 1992 the Tate Trustees announced their intention to create a separate gallery for international modern and contemporary art in London. The former Bankside Power Station was selected. Swiss architects Herzog & De Meuron were appointed to convert the building into a gallery as their proposal retained much of the original character of the building.

The iconic power station which was built in two phases between 1947 and 1963, was designed by Sir Giles Gilbert Scott. It consisted of a stunning turbine hall, 35 metres high and 152 metres long, with the boiler house alongside it and a single central chimney.

Since it opened in May 2000, more than 40 million people have visited Tate Modern. It is one of the UK's top three tourist attractions and generates an estimated £100 million in economic benefits to London each year.

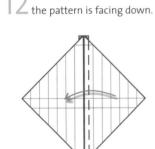

14 Fold the right side over to the left as shown.

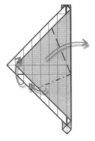

15 Fold the lower section back up along the fold made in step 9. At the same time fold the upper layer over.

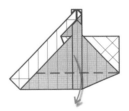

16 Fold the front layer down as shown.

tate modern continued

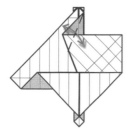

17 Fold and unfold where indicated.

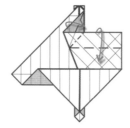

18 Fold the edge down this will reverse the fold made in the previous step.

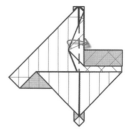

19 Carefully fold the corner over as indicated.

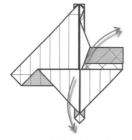

20 Unfold the last few steps back to step 15.

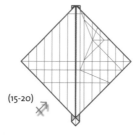

(15-20)

21 Repeat steps 15 to 21 on the other side.

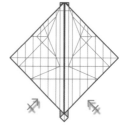

22 Now carefully re-fold steps 15-21 on both sides.

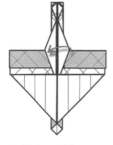

23 Fold the middle section over from the right.

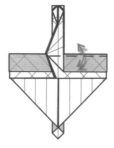

24 Fold and unfold the edge slightly below the upper edge as above.

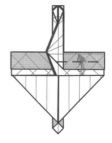

25 Fold the lower edge up to meet the crease made in the previous step.

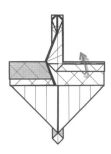

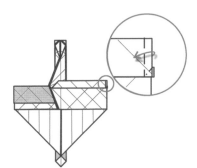

26 Fold the edge up along the crease made in step 25

27 Fold outer edge over causing a small triangular fold on the layer beneath.

28 The completed fold will look like this.

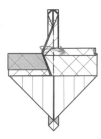

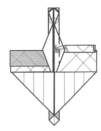

(24-31)

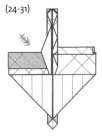

29 Fold the edge back over as indicated.

30 Fold the corner back over aligned with the folded section beneath.

31 Repeat steps 24 to 31 on the other side.

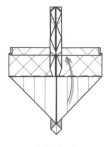

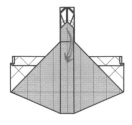

32 Now fold the lower section back up.

33 Fold the top point of the upper layer down.

34 Fold the layer down where indicated.

tate modern continued

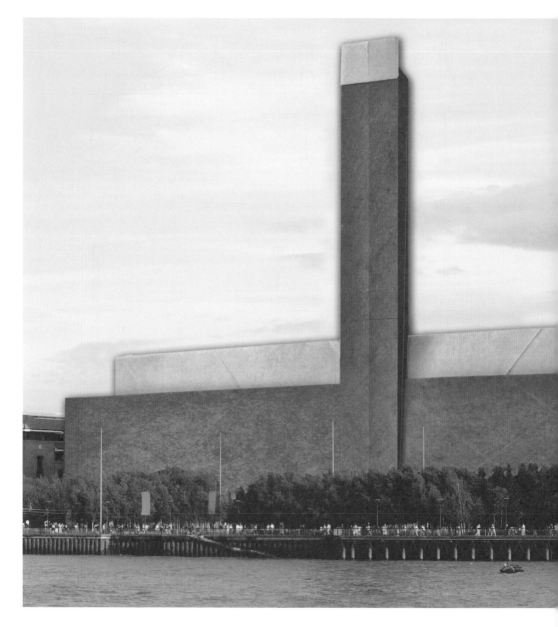

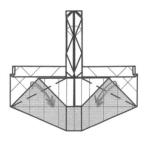

35 Fold the corners of the front layer in.

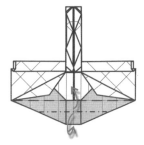

36 Fold the lower section up and down again to make a base for the model to stand on.

37 Turn the model over, it is now complete

buckingham palace

Buckingham Palace has been the official London residence of Britain's sovereigns since 1837 and today is the administrative headquarters of the Monarch. It has 775 rooms, including 19 state rooms, 52 Royal and guest bedrooms, 188 staff bedrooms, 92 offices and 78 bathrooms.

1 Start with a 2 x 1 rectangle coloured side up. Fold and unfold along the middle.

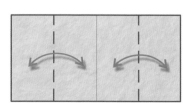

2 Fold and unfold both the left and right edges to meet the middle crease.

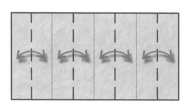

3 Fold and unfold between the creases made previously. This divides the paper into eight.

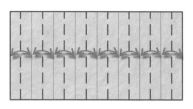

4 Fold and unfold between the creases previously made. This divides the paper into sixteen sections.

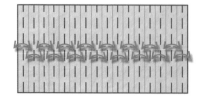

5 Fold and unfold between the creases made previously. This will divide the paper into thirty two sections.

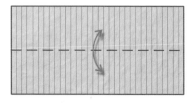

6 Now fold and unfold the paper horizontally along the middle.

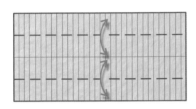

7 Fold and unfold the top and bottom edges to the middle crease.

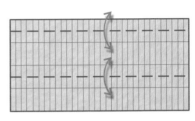

8 Fold and unfold between the creases made in the previous step.

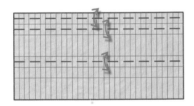

9 Fold and unfold between the creases made in the previous step.

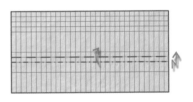

10 Fold the paper up and down along the creases made previously. This will form a pleat.

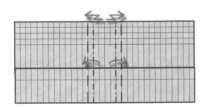

11 Make two pleats in the position shown either side of the middle section.

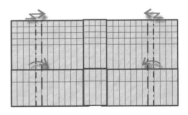

12 Fold the sides in and out again making a pleat on either side.

buckingham palace continued

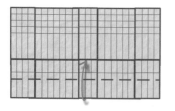

13 Fold the lower edge up to touch the folded edge above.

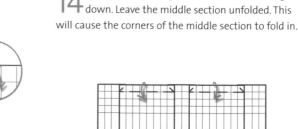

14 Fold the left and right sides of the lower edge down. Leave the middle section unfolded. This will cause the corners of the middle section to fold in.

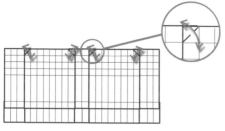

15 Turn the model over. Fold and unfold the outer corners of the upper edge.

16 Fold the two middle sections of the upper edge down. Leave the middle and outer edge unfolded.

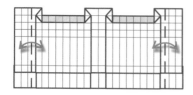

17 Fold and unfold the outer edges between the creases where indicated.

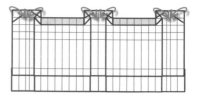

18 Fold the outer corners of the three sections in where indicated.

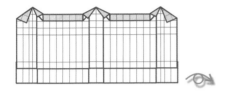

19 Now turn the model over so the patterned side faces upwards.

George IV, on his accession in 1820, decided to reconstruct the house into a pied-à-terre, using it for the same purpose as his father. As work progressed, the King had a change of heart. With the assistance of his architect, John Nash, he set about transforming the house into a palace.

Nash retained the main block but doubled its size by adding a new suite of rooms on the garden side facing west. Faced with Bath stone, the style reflected the French neo-classical influence favoured by George IV.

The rooms that were remodelled are the State and semi-State Rooms, which remain virtually unchanged since Nash's time.

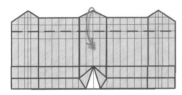

20 Fold the top section down as indicated by the arrow and the fold line.

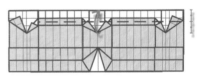

21 Fold the top section back up so that it meets the upper folded edge.

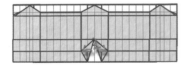

22 Fold the edges of the lower section out. This will cause the top of this section to fold over slightly. Turn the model over.

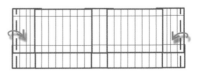

23 Fold both the left and right outer edges of the model in.

buckingham palace continued

24 Fold the outer edges in again. Then fold several pleats in the model to shape the front.

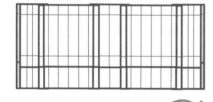

25 Turn the model over, flatten all the pleats made in the previous step.

Queen Victoria was the first sovereign to take up residence in July 1837, just three weeks after her accession, and in June 1838 she was the first British sovereign to leave from Buckingham Palace for a Coronation. Her marriage to Prince Albert in 1840 soon showed up the Palace's shortcomings. A serious problem for the newly married couple was the absence of any nurseries and too few bedrooms for visitors. The only solution was to move the Marble Arch - it now stands at the north-east corner of Hyde Park - and build a fourth wing, thereby creating a quadrangle.

The present forecourt of the Palace, where Changing the Guard takes place, was formed in 1911, as part of the Victoria Memorial scheme. The gates and railings were also completed in 1911. The North-Centre Gate is now the everyday entrance to the Palace, whilst the Central Gate is used for State occasions and the departure of the guard after Changing the Guard.

big ben

The name Big Ben is often used to describe the tower, the clock and the bell but the name was first given to the Great Bell. The tower was completed in 1859, the clock was started on 31 May and bell's strikes heard for the first time on 11 July.

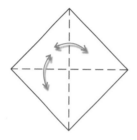

1 Start with a square coloured side down. Fold and unfold the square diagonally.

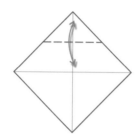

2 Fold and unfold the corner to the middle of the square.

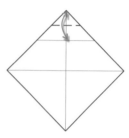

3 Fold and unfold the corner in to touch the crease made in the previous step.

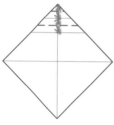

4 Fold and unfold between the creases made previously.

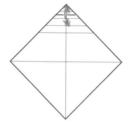

5 Fold and unfold between the creases made previously.

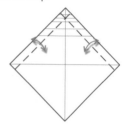

6 Fold and unfold the outer edges in. The fold should touch the creases made in step 5.

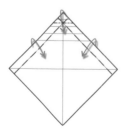

7 Fold the edges in together. This causes the top section to fold into a preliminary base shape.

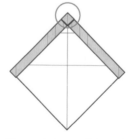

8 The next steps will show detail of the folds in the top section.

9 Fold and unfold the lower edges to the middle.

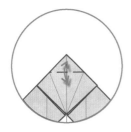

10 Fold and unfold the top section between the creases.

11 Fold the lower corner up along the crease made previously this will cause the edges to fold in.

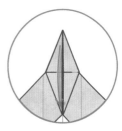

12 Now neatly Fold the point back down.

13 Sink fold the top corner into the model.

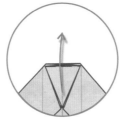

14 Carefully fold the point back up again.

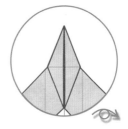

15 Your model should now resemble the illustration above. Turn it over, before continuing.

16 Fold the upper edge down and open out the paper beneath. Section completed.

17 This section is now finished and should like this.

A terrible fire destroyed most of the Palace of Westminster in 1834. Architects were invited to submit their designs for the new Palace and a commission was set up to select the best. Out of 97 designs submitted, the architect Sir Charles Barry's was successful. However, his winning design did not feature a clock tower. He added this to his design in 1836.

big ben continued

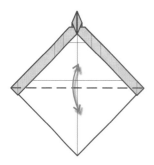

18 Turn the model over, fold and unfold along the middle.

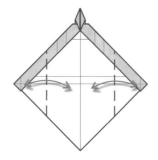

19 Fold and unfold the outer corners to the middle

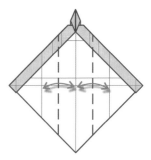

20 Fold and unfold between the creases made previously.

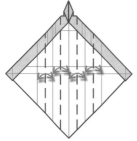

21 Fold and unfold between the creases made previously.

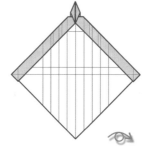

22 Turn the model over, without rotating it.

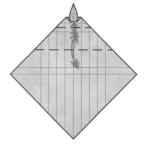

23 Fold and unfold lengthwise between the creases.

Construction of the Clock Tower began in September 1843, it was built from the inside outwards, meaning that no scaffolding was visible on the outside. All the materials were transported by river and a winch lifted materials to the masons and bricklayers. Materials for the Clock Tower came from all over the United Kingdom, cast iron girders from Regent's Canal Ironworks, Yorkshire Anston stone and Cornish granite.

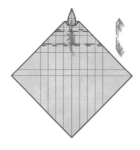

24 Fold up and down along the creases made previously causing two pleated folds.

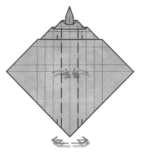

25 Once again fold the sides in and out, making two pleated folds.

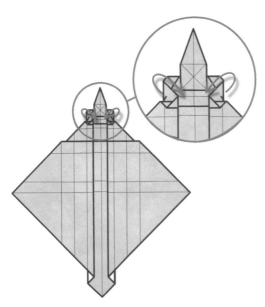
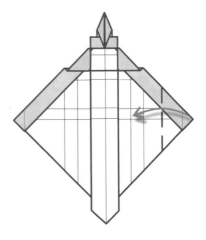

26 Fold the outer corners of the top section over to shape the tower.

27 Turn the model over. Fold the outer corner in so that the corner touches the crease indicated.

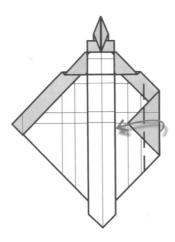
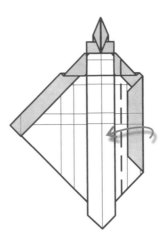

28 Fold the edge in to touch the folded edge in the middle section.

29 Now carefully fold the outer edge in to meet the centre crease line.

big ben continued

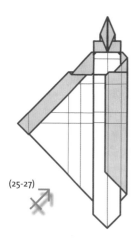

(25-27)

30 Repeat steps 25 to 27 on the other side.

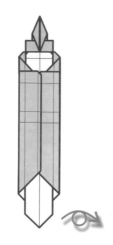

31 Now turn the model over to work on the other side.

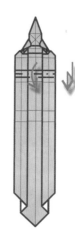

32 Fold the model up and down making a pleat where indicated by the arrow.

33 Repeat the pleating process at roughly three evenly spaced intervals.

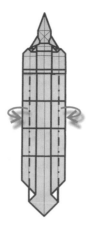

34 Fold the edges of the lower section behind. Leave the outer edges of the top section unfolded.

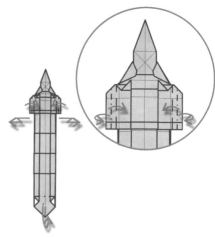

35 Fold the edges of the top section in and out again making two pleats. Then fold the lower corner behind.

the tower of london

The White Tower, which gives the entire castle its name, was built by William the Conqueror in 1078, the castle was used as a prison since 1100, but its main purpose was as a palace.

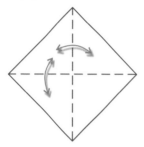

1 Start with a square coloured side down. Fold and unfold the square diagonally.

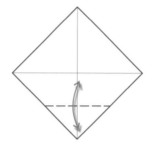

2 Fold and unfold the corner to the middle of the square.

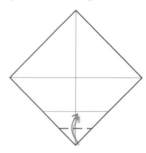

3 Fold between the lower corner and the crease made previously.

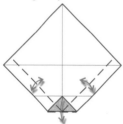

4 Fold and unfold the lower outer edges in, then unfold back to a square as shown.

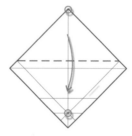

5 Fold the top corner over. The upper tip should touch the intersection of the creases below.

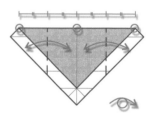

6 Fold and unfold the edges in to the middle where indicated. Then turn the model over.

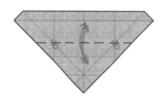

7 Fold and unfold where indicated. The fold should cut through the intersection of the creases where shown.

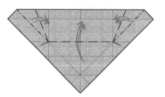

8 Fold the outer edges in. This will cause the lower section to fold up along the crease made previously.

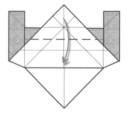

9 Fold the front corner down. The fold should align with the crease in the layer below.

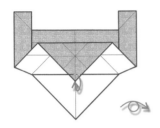

10 Fold the tip of the corner behind. Turn the model over.

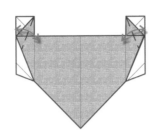

11 Fold and unfold the top left and right corners.

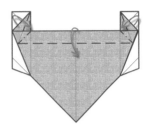

12 Fold the upper edge down between the creases made previously. This will cause the corners to refold.

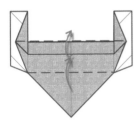

13 Fold the top edge back. Then fold the lower corner up.

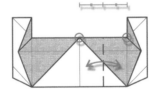

14 Fold and unfold between the edge of the turret and the middle crease.

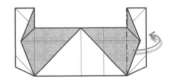

15 Fold the outer section on the right behind.

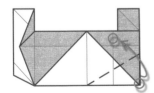

16 Fold the lower corner up between the middle crease and the outer edge. The corner should touch the crease.

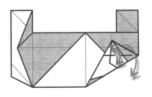

17 Fold the edge down to the folded edge. Unfold, and open out the point.

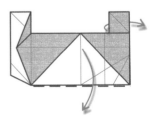

18 Fold the corner down and fold the turret out from behind.

the tower of london continued

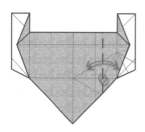

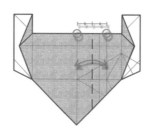

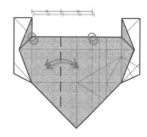

19 Fold and unfold where indicated. The crease should cut through the creases where indicated.

20 Fold and unfold in between the two creases.

21 Fold and unfold between the two creases.

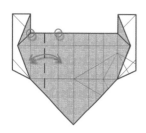

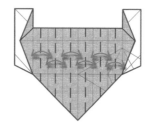

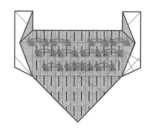

22 Fold and unfold in between the creases where indicated.

23 Fold and unfold in between the creases indicated. This will divide the section into 12.

24 Fold and unfold in between the creases indicated. This will divide the section into 24.

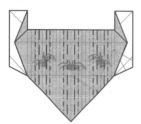

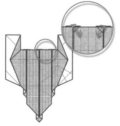

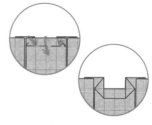

25 Fold along the creases made previously to make three sections where the folded edges touch.

26 Fold and unfold the outer corners of the upper edge.

27 Fold the edge down. This will cause the outer corners to fold in. Repeat this on the other similar sections of the upper edge.

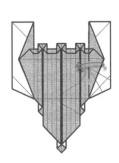

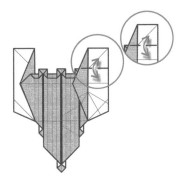

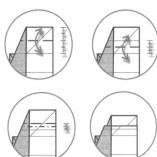

28 Fold the edge over as indicated.

29 Fold and unfold the top of the turret.

30 Fold and unfold where indicated. then fold the edge behind and up forming a pleat.

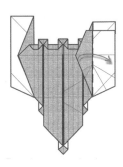

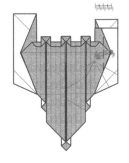

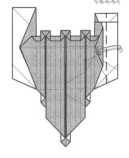

31 Fold the section back over as indicated.

32 Fold the edge over to meet the crease indicated..

33 Fold the right hand outer edge over.

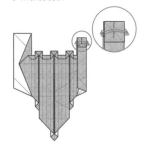

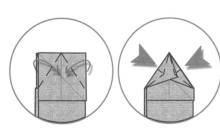

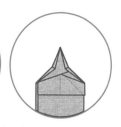

34 Make a vertical crease along the middle of the top section of the turret.

35 Fold the outer corners in. Pinch the top to form a small spire.

The right hand turret is now complete. Repeat steps 28 to 35 on the left hand turret.

the tower of london continued

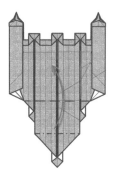

36 Fold the lower section up and back again. Turn the model over.

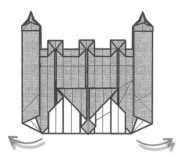

37 Use the folded corner as a stand. If the structure of the model makes the base finish smaller than the top, hold either side of the lower edge and ease it apart slightly.

The Tower has served variously as an armoury, a treasury, a menagerie, the home of the Royal Mint, a public records office, and the home of the Crown Jewels of the United Kingdom. From the early 14th century until the reign of Charles II, a procession would be led from the Tower to Westminster Abbey on the coronation of a monarch. In the absence of the monarch, the Constable of the Tower is in charge of the castle. This was a powerful and trusted position in the medieval period. In the late 15th century the castle was the prison of the Princes in the Tower. Under the Tudors, the Tower became used less as a royal residence, and despite attempts to refortify and repair the castle its defences lagged behind developments to deal with artillery. The peak period of the castle's use as a prison was the 16th and 17th centuries, when many figures who had fallen into disgrace, such as Elizabeth I before she became queen, were held within its walls. This use has led to the phrase "sent to the Tower". Despite its enduring reputation as a place of torture and death, popularised by 16th-century religious propagandists and 19th-century writers, only seven people were executed within the Tower. Today the Tower is one of the country's most popular tourist attractions and a protected World Heritage site.

the london eye

The London Eye on the banks of the River Thames is the tallest ferris wheel in Europe, and one of Londons most popular tourist attractions.

PART ONE: THE BASE Start with a square coloured side down.

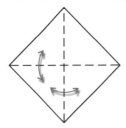

1 Fold and unfold the square in half diagonally.

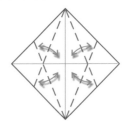

2 Fold and unfold the lower edges to the middle.

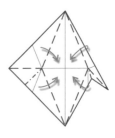

3 Fold in the lower and upper edges to the middle together. The right side shows this process in action.

4 Turn the model over. Fold in half along the centre crease.

5 Rotate the model 90 degrees anti-clockwise.

6 Fold the outer point over. Open the layers and flatten.

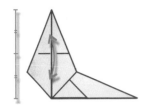

7 Fold and then unfold the section in half to form a crease in the middle.

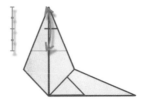

8 Fold the point down to the crease that was made in the previous step.

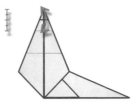

9 Fold the top corner down to touch the crease made in the previous step.

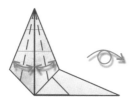

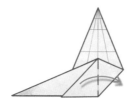

(7-12)

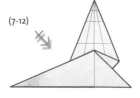

10 Fold and unfold the edges to the middle. Then turn the model over.

11 Fold the corner on the front layer over.

12 Repeat steps 7 to 12 on the other side of the model.

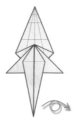

13 Fold the front layer down causing the outer edges to fold in.

14 Now turn the model over from left to right.

The wheel's 32 sealed and air-conditioned ovoidal passenger capsules are attached to the external circumference of the wheel and rotated by electric motors. Each capsule represents one of the London Boroughs, weighs 10 tonnes and holds 25 people, who are free to walk around inside the capsule, though seating is provided. The wheel rotates at 26 cm (10 in) per second (about 0.9 km/h or 0.6 mph) so that one revolution takes about 30 minutes. It does not usually stop to take on passengers; the rotation rate is slow enough to allow passengers to walk on and off the moving capsules at ground level. It is, however, stopped to allow disabled or elderly passengers time to embark and disembark safely.

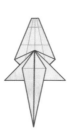

15 Fold the tip of the front layer over. Turn the model over.

16 Base part complete and ready for assembley.

the london eye continued

PART TWO: THE WHEEL Start with a square coloured side down.

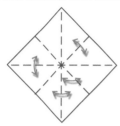

1 Fold the square in half lengthwise and diagonally.

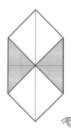

2 Fold the corner to the middle. Turn the model over.

3 Fold the outer edges to the centre crease.

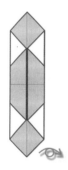

4 Turn the model over from left to right .

5 Fold the outer edges to the centre crease.

6 Fold and unfold the outer corners to the middle.

7 Fold over the top and bottom corners as indicated.

8 Now turn the model over left to right.

9 Fold in half lengthwise as indicated.

10 Fold and unfold the outer lower corners.

11 Fold and unfold between the lower edge and the creases made in the previous step.

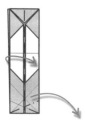

12 Refold the crease from the previous step and fold the front layer down.

13 Fold the edge behind. Repeat steps 10 to 14 where indicated.

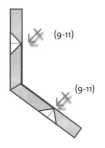

14 Repeat steps 9 to 11 where indicated.

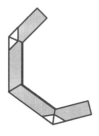

15 One section is complete. Now make two more.

The wheel was constructed in sections which were floated up the Thames on barges and assembled lying flat on piled platforms in the river. Once the wheel was complete it was lifted into an upright position by a strand jack system. It was first raised at 2 degrees per hour until it reached 65 degrees, then left in that position for a week while engineers prepared for the second phase of the lift. The total weight of steel in the Eye is 1,700 tonnes (1,870 short tons). The project was European with major components coming from six countries: the steel was supplied from the UK and fabricated in The Netherlands, the cables came from Italy, the bearings came from Germany, the spindle and hub were cast in the Czech Republic, the capsules were made in France and the glass for these came from Italy and the electrical components from the UK. The London Eye was formally opened by the then Prime Minister, Tony Blair, on 31 December 1999.

the london eye continued

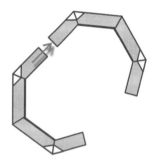 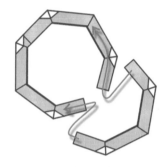 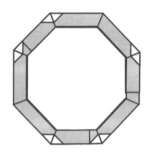

16 Join two units together by inserting the end of one unit into another.

17 To insert the third unit, open one end of the assembly and insert two segments. Then refold, producing an octagonal ring.

18 The wheel is complete, set aside until you are ready to assemble the model.

PART THREE: THE GONDOLAS These are made from smaller squares, a quarter size if the base and wheel squares.

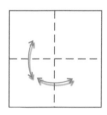 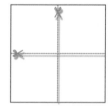 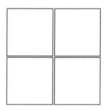

1 Fold and unfold the square in half lengthwise

2 Cut the square to make four smaller squares.

3 This will make four gondolas. You will need seven.

 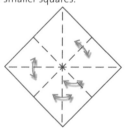 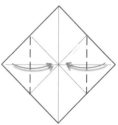

4 Start with a smaller square. Rotate 90 degrees.

5 Fold and unfold the square, lengthwise and diagonally.

6 Fold the outer corners to the middle crease line.

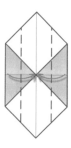

7 Fold the outer edges to the middle line.l

8 Fold the lower point of the model up.

9 Fold the lower outer cornersin to the middle.

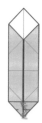

10 Fold and unfold lower point of the model as shown.

11 Fold and unfold diagonally where indicated.

12 Fold the top section down and reverse fold the upper edges inside.

13 Fold and unfold where indicated.

14 Fold the front layer up to touch the crease made in the previous step.

15 Fold and unfold the edges to the middle.

the london eye continued

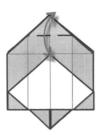

16 Fold and unfold where indicated.

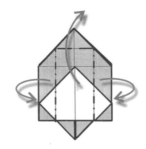

17 Fold the front layer up along the crease made previously. This will cause the edges to fold in.

18 Fold the lower point of the model behind.

19 Fold and unfold along the line indicated.

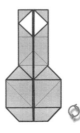

20 Rotate the model 90 degrees.

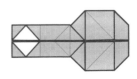

21 The gondola is now complete, you need to make seven gondolas in total.

PART FOUR: ASSEMBLING THE LONDON EYE

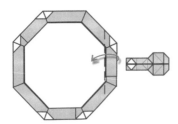

1 Open up the outer edge by folding the edge over.

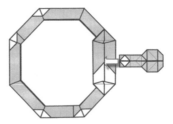

2 Insert the end into the pocket. Align the edge of the pocket with the edge of the white diamond.

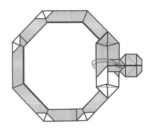

3 Fold the edge back to lock the pod in place.

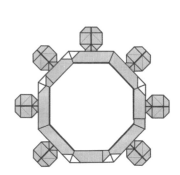

4 Add six more pods to complete the wheel.

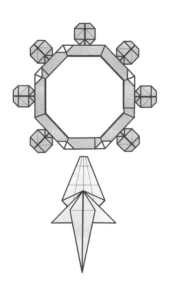

5 Start with the wheel and the base.

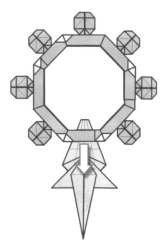

6 Place the assembled wheel onto the base as shown.

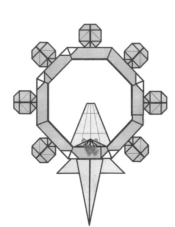

7 Fold the corners of the inner section over the upper edge of the wheel.

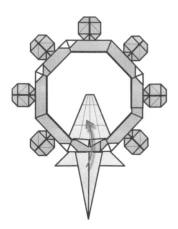

8 Fold the point back up over the section of the wheel.

9 Now turn the model over left to right.

the london eye continued

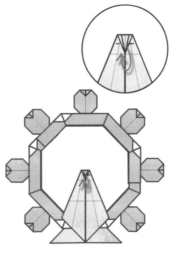

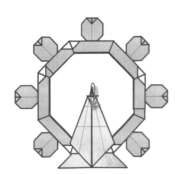

10 Fold the tip of the base over the folded egde.

11 Fold the tip of the point behind to lock the layers together.

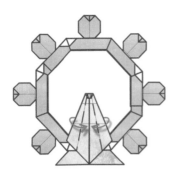

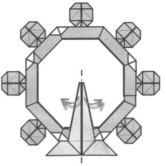

12 Fold the edges of the front layer in to the middle. Turn the model over.

13 Fold the base along the middle this will strengthen the model and should enable it to stand.

tower bridge

At 244 metres in length and with two towers each 65 metres high, Tower Bridge is one of the most famous bridges in the world.

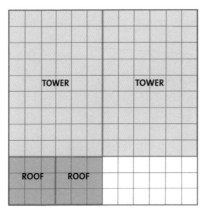

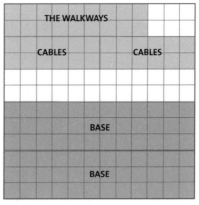

Tower bridge is made from several pieces that can be made from two squares of paper. The diagrams above show the proportions of each of the pieces. Simply fold and crease your squares of paper into a 12 x 12 grid, then cut along the crease lines to make the correct size pieces.

PART ONE: THE BASE You will need two 9 x 6 rectangles.

1 Start with one 9x6 rectangle, fold and unfold between the creases where indicated.

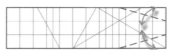

2 Fold and unfold the corners in between the mid creases and the fold made previously.

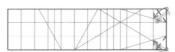

3 Fold the corners in to the crease made previously.

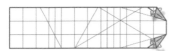

4 Fold the edges over again to the crease made in step 2.

5 Now fold the top and bottom right hand corners in again.

6 Fold and unfold two diagonal folds in the middle, then fold the outer edge.

7 Fold and unfold between the creases indicated partway down the length of the model.

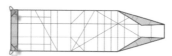

8 Fold over the outer corners to the creases made previously.

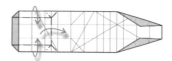

9 Fold the outer section over. At the same time fold the edges in along the crease made in step 7.

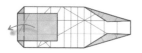

10 Fold the folded section over again.

11 Fold the right side over. The end should touch the edge of the folded section on the other side.

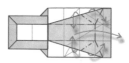

12 Fold the section back again. At the same time fold in the edges where indicated.

13 Turn the model over and then fold the edge over.

14 Make to diagonal folds where indicated.

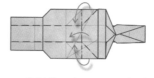

15 Fold the edges perpendicular. to the base. As well as folding the right section up along the creases made previously.

16 Fold the left side section up to be perpendicular to the base of the model.

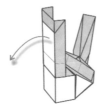

17 Now fold the left side section down as indicated.

Construction started in 1886 and took eight years. Two massive piers, containing over 70,000 tons of concrete, were sunk into the riverbed to support the bridge. More than 11,000 tons of steel for the framework of the towers and walkways.

tower bridge continued

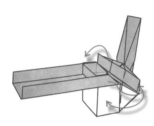  

18 Fold the edges of the right side section around the middle shape. At the same time tuck the edge of the middle section beneath the folded edge.

19 Fold the section down and open out the edges.

20 Base section complete. You will need one base section for each tower.

PART TWO: THE TOWERS You will need two 9 x 6 rectangles.

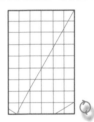 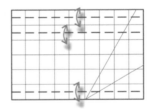 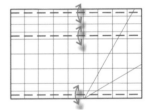

1 Start with one of the 9 x 6 rectangles, rotate it 90 degrees.

2 Fold and unfold between the creases indicated.

3 Fold and unfold again between the creases indicated.

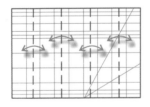 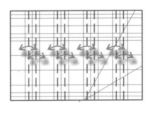 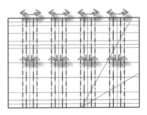

4 Continue to fold and unfold between the creases indicated.

5 Fold and unfold between the creases indicated.

6 Fold sections in and out again to form four pleated sections. Turn the model over.

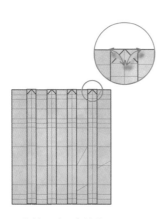

7 Fold and unfold the upper corners of the folded sections, see detail. Turn the model over.

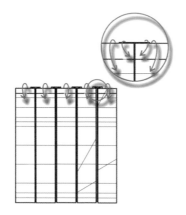

8 Fold the top edges over, at the same time re-fold the folds made prevously to make some folded triangles along the top edge.

9 Fold the middle section down and up again to make a pleat. Then fold the lower edge up.

10 Now fold the left hand edge over as indicated.

11 Fold the edge over. and tuck it in under the folded section.

12 Push the edges in to make an even 3D four sided tower.

13 One tower is complete, you will need to mske one more.

When it was built, Tower Bridge was the largest and most sophisticated bascule bridge ever completed (bascule comes from the French for see-saw). These bascules were operated by hydraulics, using steam to power the enormous pumping engines. The energy created was stored in six massive accumulators, as soon as power was required to lift the Bridge, it was always readily available. The accumulators fed the driving engines, which drove the bascules up and down. Despite the complexity of the system, the bascules only took about a minute to raise to their maximum angle of 86 degrees. Today, the bascules are still operated by hydraulic power, but since 1976 they have been driven by oil and electricity rather than steam.

tower bridge continued

PART THREE: THE ROOF You will need two 3 x 3 squares, coloured side up.

1 Fold and unfold the square in half lengthwise. Then turn the model over.

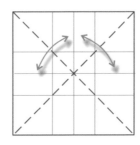

2 Fold and unfold the square in half diagonally.

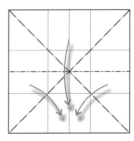

3 Re fold the creases made previously to make a waterbomb base.

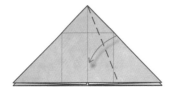

4 Fold the outer edge in to the middle crease.

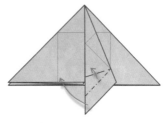

5 Fold the front layer up. the base of the triangle shape is level with the crease in the layer beneath.

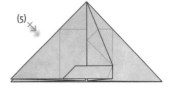

6 Repeat step 5 on the opposite side of the model.

7 Tuck the upper edge of the lower section into the folded edge in the upper section to link them together.

8 Turn the model over and repeat steps 4 to 7 on the other side.

9 Open the model to make the shape of a pyramid, the roof is now complete. You will need to make one more.

PART FOUR: THE WALKWAYS You will need the 9 x 2 rectangle, coloured side up

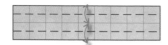

1 Fold and unfold the outer edges to the middle.

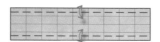

2 Fold and unfold between the outer edge and the crease made previously.

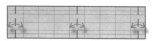

3 Fold and unfold between the creases indicated.

4 Fold and unfold between the creases indicated.

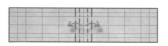

5 Fold along the crease made previously to make a raised section in the middle.

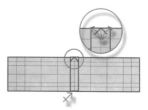

6 Fold and unfold the outer corners of the folded section on the upper and lower corners.

7 Turn over then fold the top and bottom edges in as indicated.

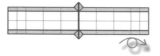

8 Fold over the corners of the folded section behind to make two triangular points. Turn over.

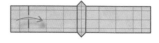

9 Fold one end in where indicated.

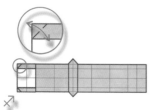

10 Fold and unfold the outer corners as indicated in detail.

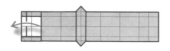

11 Fold the left hand edge back over between the creases.

In 1952, the bridge opened while a number 78 bus was crossing. The bus was near the edge of the south bascule when it started to rise, driver Albert Gunter made a decision to accelerate, clearing a 3 ft gap to drop 6 ft onto the north bascule, which had not yet started to rise.

tower bridge continued

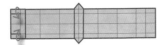

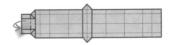

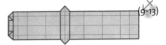

12 Fold the edges of the section in. Refold the folds made in step 11 and squash the corner of the layer beneath.

13 Fold the outer left hand edge behind.

14 Repeat steps 10 to 14 on the other side.

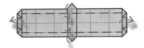

15 Fold the edges in to be perpendicular to the base. This will form a box shape.

16 Fold the lower folded edges out to be level with the edge of the upper edges.

17 The top section is now complete.

PART FIVE: THE CABLE You will need the 6 x 2 rectangles, coloured side up

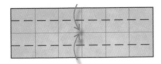

1 Fold the outer edges to the middle.

2 Now neatly fold both the edges out again.

3 Turn the model over so that the printed side is facing down.

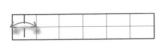

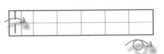

4 Fold and unfold the outer edge to the crease.

5 Fold the outer edge in to the crease. Then fold it perpendicular to the model. Turn the model over.

6 The cable is now complete. You will need one set for each tower.

ASSEMBLING TOWER BRIDGE

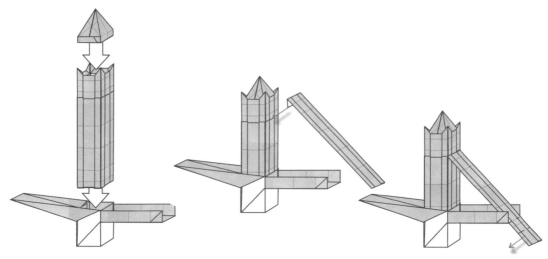

1 Insert the roof into the tower. Then insert the tower into the base section.

2 Insert the vertical edge of each of the cables into the pocket created by the folded edge on the outer side of each of the towers.

3 Align the cables with the edge of the model. then make a fold where the sections touch. Then fold the edge in to touch the folded edge.

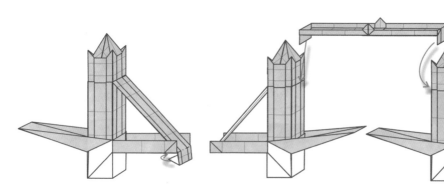

4 Tuck the folded edge into the pocket in the section above. Make two towers and align them opposite each other.

5 Finally insert the vertical folded edges of the walkway as far as they will go into the pockets created by the folds on the inner

face of each tower. Adjust and align the towers as necessary until the bascules are in alignment with each other.

tower bridge continued

Officially opened on 30 June 1894 Tower bridge is 800 feet (244 m) in length with two towers each 213 feet (65 m) high, built on piers. The central span of 200 feet (61 m) between the towers is split into two equal bascules or leaves, which can be raised to an angle of 83 degrees to allow river traffic to pass. The bascules, weighing over 1,000 tons each, are counterbalanced to minimise the force required and allow raising in five minutes.

The two side-spans are suspension bridges, each 270 feet (82 m) long, with the suspension rods anchored both at the abutments and through rods contained within the bridge's upper walkways. The pedestrian walkways are 143 feet (44 m) above the river at high tide.

The high-level open air walkways between the towers gained an unpleasant reputation as a haunt for unsavoury characters and were closed in 1910. In 1982 they were reopened as part of the Tower Bridge Exhibition, an exhibition now housed in the bridge's twin towers, the high-level walkways and the Victorian engine rooms. The walkways, which are now enclosed, boast stunning views of the River Thames and many famous London sites.

tower of london ravens

Legend says that the kingdom and the Tower will fall if the six resident ravens ever leave the fortress. Their lodgings are to be found next to the Wakefield Tower.

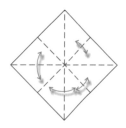

1 Start with a square coloured side down. Fold and unfold in half lengthwise and diagonally.

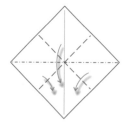

2 Fold the edges in along the lengthwise folds and reverse fold the diagonal folds.

3 Fold the outer edges to the middle. Then fold over the upper triangle. Then unfold.

4 Fold the front layer up along the upper crease. This will cause the edges to fold in.

(3-4)

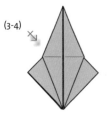

5 Repeat steps 3 to 4 behind.

6 Fold the side of the front layer over. At the same time fold the top point down and right.

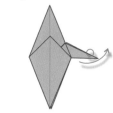

7 Hold the point and slide it up slightly.

(6-7)

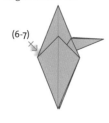

8 Repeat steps 6 to 7 behind.

9 Fold and unfold the top layer of the points in half.

10 Fold the base of the points behind and refold the upper layer of the points in half.

11 Now turn the model over.

12 Fold the upper layer of the points in half.

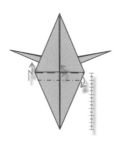

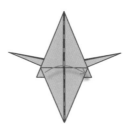

13 Fold the top layer of the lower section of the model up.

14 Fold the lower section up and down again. The down fold should be about ⅛th of the length.

15 Now carefully fold the model in half.

16 Rotate the model 90 degrees.

17 Hold the tip and slide it up.

18 Reverse fold the tip to make a head.

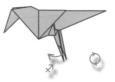

19 Reverse fold the legs up and down again. Repeat behind.

20 Reverse fold the tips of the points back and then forward to make feet. Repeat behind.

london telephone box

The red telephone box was the result of a competition in 1924 to design a kiosk that would be acceptable to all the London Metropolitan Boroughs.

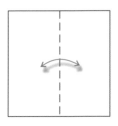

1 Fold and unfold the square lengthwise.

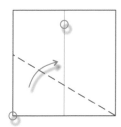

2 Fold the lower corner up so that the corner touches the folded line. The fold should extend from the opposite corner.

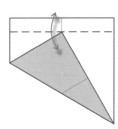

3 Fold and unfold the upperedge over the folded point.

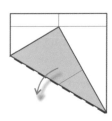

4 Unfold the folded triangle. Rotate the model 90 degrees clockwise.

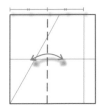

5 Fold and unfold the outer edge over to the crease.

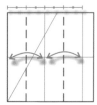

6 Fold and unfold between the creases where indicated.

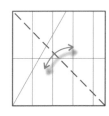

7 Fold and unfold the square diagonally.

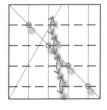

8 Fold and unfold along the lines where the diagonal crease touch the vertical creases.

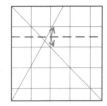

9 Fold and unfold between the creases where indicated.

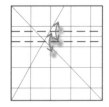

10 Fold and unfold between the creases where indicated.

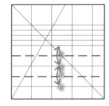

11 Fold and unfold between the creases where indicated.

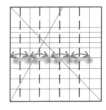

12 Fold and unfold between the creases where indicated.

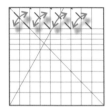

13 Fold and unfold four diagonal folds in the upper four sections of the model.

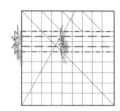

14 Fold the edges the upper and lower section in forming two pleats.

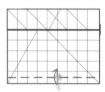

15 Fold up the lower edge to the crease.

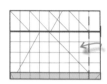

16 Fold the outer edge in where indicated.

17 Fold the outer edge in where indicated.

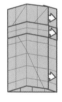

18 Fold the other side over and tuck into the folded side opposite.

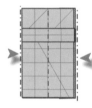

19 Push the edges in to make an even 3D four sided shape.

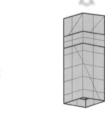

20 The next step shows a viewpoint from the top.

21 Fold the smaller section down, causing a diagonal fold creased previously in the adjacent section.

22 Fold the next section over diagonally. This will cause the adjacent section to fold diagonally.

23 Continue the process of folding over the diagonal folds.

24 Continue the process of folding over the diagonal folds.

london telephone box continued

25 Fold the last corner over and tuck it into the model between the space between the folded corners.

26 Fold the four corners of thetop section in.

27 Fold the top rim in slightly to shape the top of the model.

tower of london beefeater

The Yeomen Warders of Her Majesty's Royal Palace and Fortress the Tower of London, popularly known as the Beefeaters, are ceremonial guardians of the Tower of London.

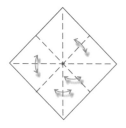

1 Fold the square in half diagonally and lengthwise .

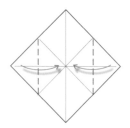

2 Fold the corner to the middle.

3 Fold the edges in again.

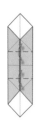

4 Fold and unfold the model where indicated.

5 Fold and unfold the lower corner diagonally as shown.

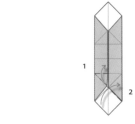

6 Fold the upper layer up at 1 open the point and fold over the edge at 2.

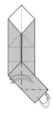

7 Fold the section over, this will cause the lower edge to fold up.

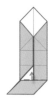

8 Fold out the paper from the layer beneath.

9 Fold the lower section up, open the layers and flatten.

10 Fold the corner of the lower section down to the bottom.

11 Fold the corner up, open the layers and flatten them.

12 Fold and unfold the edges of the section to the middle.

tower of london beefeater continued

   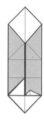

13 Fold the section over re-folding the folds made the step 12.

14 Fold the point back over to the right.

15 Now carefully fold the section in half.

16 Repeat steps 11 to 15 on the other side.

17 Fold the lower corner up as shown.

18 Fold the edges of the lower section in to the middle.

19 Fold out the trapped paper.

20 Fold the tip down and up again to form a nose shape.

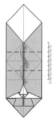 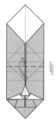 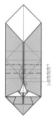 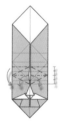

21 Fold and unfold between the creases where indicated.

22 Fold and unfold between the creases where indicated.

23 Fold and unfold between the creases where indicated.

24 Fold the top section down and up. At the same time fold the upper layers out on both sides where indicated.

25 Fold the upper section down and up again where indicated.

26 Fold the upper corner down.

27 Fold the corner up as indicated.

28 Fold the edges of the upper section in. This will cause the paper in the lower layer to fold in.

29 Fold the edge of the hat up and the edges of the hat in and fold the corner of the badge over.

30 Fold and unfold the corners of the middle section.

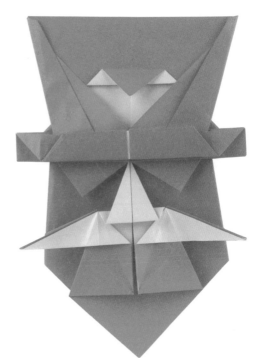

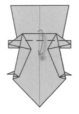

31 Fold the edges of the lower section in, this will cause the paper in the layer beneath to fold in.

32 Fold the edge over, the model is now complete.

useful website addresses

cleopatras needle
www.historic-uk.com/HistoryUK/HistoryofBritain

the monument
www.themonument.info/

the shard
http://the-shard.com

the gherkin
http://www.30stmaryaxe.com/

the royal exchange
www.theroyalexchange.com

the royal albert hall
www.royalalberthall.com

the royal festival hall
www.southbankcentre.co.uk/venues/royal-festival-hall

the O2 arena
www.theo2.co.uk

westminster abbey
www.westminster-abbey.org/

st paul's cathedral
www.stpauls.co.uk/

st mary le strand
www.stmarylestrand.org/

victoria and albert museum
www.vam.ac.uk/

the tate modern
www.tate.org.uk/

buckingham palace
www.royal.gov.uk/.../buckinghampalace

big ben
www.parliament.uk/bigben

the tower of london
www.hrp.org.uk/TowerOfLondon

the london eye
www.londoneye.com/

tower bridge
www.towerbridge.org.uk/

The Papers
The next 16 pages contains all the patterns and textures used to make all the models in this book. You can cut the papers out and use them to make your models, or if you prefer you can scan the patterns and print out or photocopy them. Please note copying is limited to 30 copies of each design.

THE GHERKIN